THE
WAR WITH GERMANY

A STATISTICAL SUMMARY

940. 3

By

LEONARD P. AYRES

Colonel, General Staff

CHIEF OF THE STATISTICS BRANCH OF THE GENERAL STAFF

B 43

Second Edition with data revised to August 1, 1919

WASHINGTON
GOVERNMENT PRINTING OFFICE
1919

THE

LETTER OF INSTRUCTION.

—————

WAR DEPARTMENT,
WASHINGTON, *May 10, 1919.*

SIR: Now that the negotiations of the peace commission are draw-
ing to a close there is general desire for a stock-taking of the efforts
made and the results achieved by the United States in the war. In
addition to the other reports being prepared by the different divisions
of the War Department there is need for a statement which shall
set forth the significant facts and figures with respect to those major
steps in our military preparation and action which, taken together,
constitute the record of our participation in the war.

These main steps are not difficult to distinguish from the innumer-
able details connected with them. They include such major enterprises as raising the men, training them, transporting them overseas,
furnishing small arms, artillery, and airplanes, conducting battle
operations, and caring for the sick and wounded. It is important
that there should be available at an early date an authoritative account giving the important facts about these consecutive operations
of the war so that the more detailed reports that are beginning to
appear may be judged in their proper setting and perspective.

For these reasons I wish you would have prepared as promptly as
possible a brief and simple statistical report showing what was accomplished by the department and the cooperating agencies during
the war.

Very truly, yours,

NEWTON D. BAKER,
Secretary of War.

Col. LEONARD P. AYRES,
Chief of the Statistics Branch of the General Staff.

3

LETTER OF TRANSMISSION.

WAR DEPARTMENT,
Washington, May 31, 1919.

SIR: In accordance with your instructions there is transmitted herewith a statistical summary of the larger steps in the military preparation and action of the United States in the late war. The data presented have been compiled by the several sections of the Statistics Branch of the General Staff. In the main they set forth facts taken from the reports made by the Branch each week during the war to the President, to yourself, and to the Chief of Staff. These have been supplemented by facts and figures secured from the offices of the Statistics Branch maintained during the war at General Headquarters and at the headquarters of the Services of Supply in France. Some of the data have also been secured from the office of the Statistics Branch maintained at the headquarters of the American Commission to Negotiate Peace in Paris. Other data have been taken from the reports of the Interallied Bureau of Statistics, of which the Statistics Branch has been the American agency, and from the files of the Supreme War Council at Versailles with which the Branch has maintained close contact.

While it is still impossible to secure final figures on some points or entirely reliable ones on others, care has been taken to insure such degree of reliability in the data presented as is reasonably feasible. Since most of the data have been taken from compilations which have been currently maintained for many months, and which have been subjected to repeated checking and revision, it is believed that they are in the main fairly trustworthy.

Very truly, yours,

LEONARD P. AYRES,
Colonel, General Staff, Chief of Statistics Branch.

Hon. NEWTON D. BAKER,
Secretary of War.

TABLE OF CONTENTS.

DIAGRAMS, TABLES, AND MAPS.

LIST OF DIAGRAMS.

LIST OF TABLES.

LIST OF MAPS.

FIGURES OF AMERICAN PARTICIPATION IN THE WAR.

Total armed forces, including Army, Navy, Marine Corps, etc._ 4, 800, 000
Total men in the Army_____ 4, 000, 000
Men who went overseas_____ 2, 086, 000
Men who fought in France_____ 1, 390, 000
Greatest number sent in one month_____ 306, 000
Greatest number returning in one month_____ 333, 000
Tons of supplies shipped from America to France_____ 7, 500, 000
Total registered in draft_____ 24, 234, 021
Total draft inductions_____ 2, 810, 296
Greatest number inducted in one month_____ 400, 000
Graduates of Line Officers' Training Schools_____ 80, 568
Cost of war to April 30, 1919_____ $21, 850, 000, 000
Cost of Army to April 30, 1919_____ $13, 930, 000, 000
Battles fought by American troops_____ 13
Months of American participation in the war_____ 19
Days of battle_____ 200
Days of duration of Meuse-Argonne battle_____ 47
Americans in Meuse-Argonne battle_____ 1, 200, 000
American casualties in Meuse-Argonne battle_____ 120, 000
American battle deaths in war_____ 50, 000
American wounded in war_____ 206, 000
American deaths from disease_____ 57, 500
Total deaths in the Army_____ 115, 500

11

Chapter I.

FOUR MILLION MEN.

THE MEN WHO SERVED.

About 4,000,000 men served in the Army of the United States during the war (Apr. 6, 1917 to Nov. 11, 1918). The total number of men serving in the armed forces of the country, including the Army, the Navy, the Marine Corps, and the other services, amounted to 4,800,000. It was almost true that among each 100 American citizens 5 took up arms in defense of the country.

During the Civil War 2,400,000 men served in the northern armies or in the Navy. In that struggle 10 in each 100 inhabitants of the Northern States served as soldiers or sailors. The American effort in the war with Germany may be compared with that of the Northern States in the Civil War by noting that in the present war we raised twice as many men in actual numbers, but that in proportion to the population we raised only half as many.

It would be interesting and instructive to make comparisons between the numbers in the American armies during the present war and those of France, Great Britain, Italy, and Germany, but unfortunately this is most difficult to do fairly and truly. The reason for the difficulty lies in the diverse military policies of the nations.

It was the policy of France, for example, to mobilize and put into uniform most of the able-bodied men in the population who were not beyond middle age. Some of these were sent into the combatant forces and services of supply of the active armies. Thousands of others were put at work in munitions factories. Others worked on railroads or cultivated their farms. In general, it was the policy of the Government to put its available man power into uniform and then assign these soldiers to the work that had to be done, whether it was directly military in nature or not.

In the United States it was the policy to take into the Army only those men who were physically fit to fight and to assign them, save in exceptional cases, only to work directly related to the ordinary duties of a soldier. The work of making munitions, running railroads, and building ships was done by men not enrolled in the armed forces of the Nation.

13

The policies of the other Governments were all different from the two just described. These are the reasons why accurate international comparisons of armies will not be possible until figures are available showing the numbers and lengths of service of the men in the combatant forces of the different nations rather than the figures now at hand showing the total numbers called to the colors and placed on the rolls.

THE AMERICAN EXPEDITIONARY FORCES AND THE BRITISH EXPEDITIONARY FORCES.

There is, however, one comparison which may fairly be made. This is the comparison between the American Expeditionary Forces

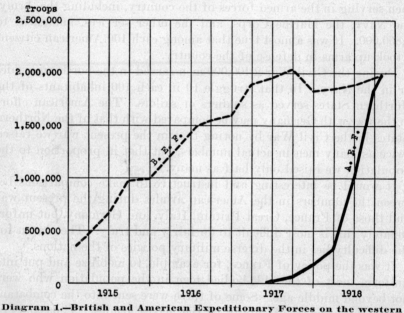

Diagram 1.—British and American Expeditionary Forces on the western front.

and the British Expeditionary Forces. Both countries devoted their major efforts to building up and maintaining their armies in France. The results are set forth in diagram 1, which shows the strength of the two forces at different dates.

The British curve mounts rapidly at first and falls off in the latter part of the period. The American starts slowly and then shoots up very rapidly. The British curve is in general convex in shape and the American is concave.

The British sent to France many more men in their first year in the war than we did in our first year. On the other hand, it took

England three years to reach a strength of 2,000,000 men in France and the United States accomplished it in one-half of that time.

It must, however, be borne in mind that the British had to use men from the beginning to fill gaps caused by casualties, while the American forces were for many months built up in strength by all the new arrivals.

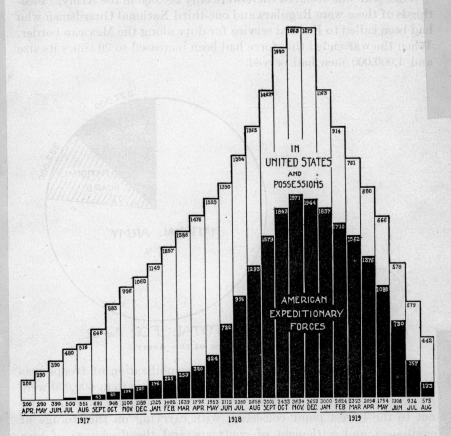

IN UNITED STATES AND POSSESSIONS

AMERICAN EXPEDITIONARY FORCES

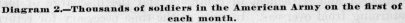

Diagram 2.—Thousands of soldiers in the American Army on the first of each month.

ARMY AT HOME AND IN FRANCE.

The most difficult feature of the American undertaking is to be found in the concentration of the major part of the effort into the few months of the spring and summer of 1918. When the country entered the war it was not anticipated in America, or suggested by France and England, that the forces to be shipped overseas should even approximate in numbers those that were actually sent.

It was not until the German drive was under way in March, 1918, that the allies called upon America for the supreme effort that carried a million and a half soldiers to France in six months. Diagram 2 shows the number of soldiers in the American Army each month from the beginning of the war and the number of them who were overseas.

When war was declared there were only 200,000 in the Army. Two-thirds of these were Regulars and one-third National Guardsmen who had been called to Federal service for duty along the Mexican border. When the war ended this force had been increased to 20 times its size and 4,000,000 men had served.

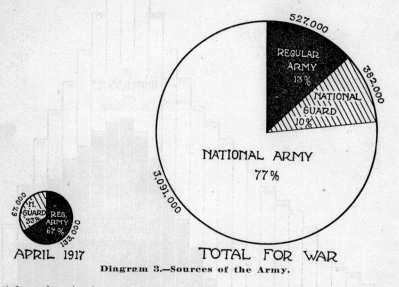

Diagram 3.—Sources of the Army.

After the signing of the armistice, demobilization of troops was begun immediately. As diagram 2 indicates, more than 600,000 were discharged during December. Forces in this country were at once cut to the lowest point consistent with carrying on the storage of equipment and settlement of contracts, and the discharge of men returning from overseas. In spite of the time necessary for return of overseas forces, demobilization was carried forward more rapidly in proportion to the number under arms than in any previous American war.

Diagram 3 shows the three sources from which the Army came.

More than half a million came in through the Regular Army. Almost 400,000 more, or nearly 10 per cent, entered through the National Guard. More than three-quarters of all came in through the selective service or National Army enlistments. Of every 100 men 10 were National Guardsmen, 13 were Regulars, and 77 belonged to the National Army, or would have if the services had not been consolidated and the distinctions wiped out on August 7, 1918.

THE SELECTIVE SERVICE.

The willingness with which the American people accepted the universal draft was the most remarkable feature in the history of our preparation for war.

It is a noteworthy evidence of the enthusiastic support given by the country to the war program that, despite previous hostility to the principle of universal liability for military service, a few months after the selective service law was passed, the standing of the drafted soldier was fully as honorable in the estimation of his companions and of the country in general as was that of the man who enlisted voluntarily. Moreover, the record of desertions from the Army shows that the total was smaller than in previous wars and a smaller percentage occurred among drafted men than among those who volunteered. The selective service law was passed on May 19, 1917, and as subsequently amended it mobilized all the man power of the Nation from the ages of 18 to 45, inclusive. Under this act, 24,234,021 men were registered and slightly more than 2,800,000 were inducted into the military service. All this was accomplished in a manner that was fair to the men, supplied the Army with soldiers as rapidly as they could be equipped and trained, and resulted in a minimum of disturbance to the industrial and economic life of the Nation.

The first registration, June 5, 1917, covered the ages from 21 to 31. The second registration, one year later (June 5, 1918 and Aug. 24, 1918), included those who had become 21 years old since the first registration. The third registration (Sept. 12, 1918), extended the age limits downward to 18 and upward to 45. The total number registered with the proportion who were actually inducted into the service is shown in Table 1.

TABLE 1.—*Men registered and inducted.*

Registration.	Age limits.	Registered.	Inducted.	Per cent inducted.
First and second	21 to 31	10,679,814	2,666,867	25
Third	18 to 20 32 to 45	13,228,762	120,157	1
Alaska, Hawaii, and Porto Rico	18 to 45	325,445	23,272	7
Total	18 to 45	24,234,021	2,810,296	12

At the outbreak of the war, the total male population of the country was about 54,000,000. During the war some 26,000,000 of them, or nearly half of all, were either registered under the selective-service act or were serving in the Army or Navy without being registered. Diagram 4 shows the percentages of the male population who were included in each of the registrations and the proportion who were not registered.

The experience of the Civil War furnishes a basis for comparing the methods used and the results obtained in the two great struggles. This comparison is strikingly in favor of the methods used in the present war. During the Civil War large sums were paid in bounties

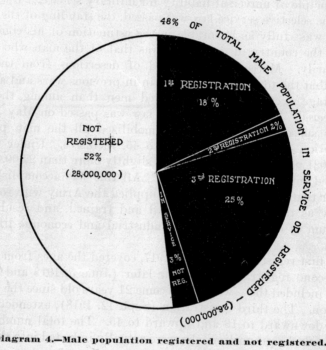

Diagram 4.—Male population registered and not registered.

in the hope that by this means recourse to the draft might be made unnecessary. This hope was frustrated and the draft was carried through by methods which were expensive and inefficient. This may be summed up by noting that during the War with Germany we raised twice as many men as we raised during the Civil War, and at one-twentieth of the cost. This does not mean one-twentieth of the cost per man, but that 20 times as much money was actually spent by the Northern States in the Civil War in recruiting their armies as was spent for the same purpose by the United States in the War with Germany. In this war 60 per cent of all armed forces were secured by the draft as compared with 2 per cent in the case of the Civil War. Diagram 5 shows the number of men inducted through the draft each month.

The columns and the figures of the diagram illustrate the manner in which the men came into the service. In the fall of 1917 the first half million came in rapidly. During the winter the accessions were relatively few, and those that did come in were largely used as

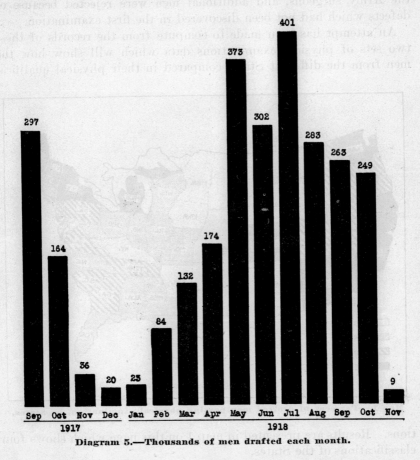

Diagram 5.—Thousands of men drafted each month.

replacements and for special services. In the spring of 1918 came the German drive and with it urgent calls from France for unlimited numbers of men. Then over a period of several months the numbers of new men brought into the service mounted into the hundreds of thousands, and reached their highest point in July, when 400,000 were inducted. During the succeeding months the numbers fell off considerably on account of the epidemic of influenza, and with November the inductions ceased entirely due to the unexpected ending of the war.

REJECTIONS FOR PHYSICAL REASONS.

Under the operation of the draft, registrants were given physical examinations by the local boards in order that those men who were not of sufficient physical soundness and vigor for military life might be sorted out. After those who were found to be qualified for service had been sent to camp, they were given another examination by the Army surgeons, and additional men were rejected because of defects which had not been discovered in the first examination.

An attempt has been made to compute from the records of these two sets of physical examinations data which will show how the men from the different States compared in their physical qualifica-

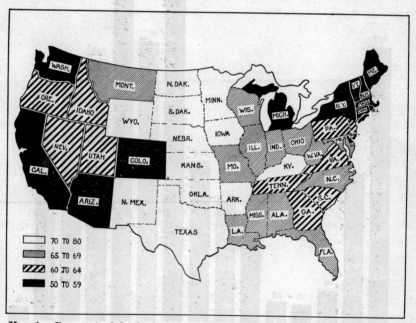

Map 1.—Per cent of drafted men passing physical examination, by States.

tions. Results are presented in map 1 on this page which shows four classifications of the States.

First come those States which are indicated in outline. These are the States which sent men of so high an order of physical condition that from 70 to 80 per cent of them survived the two examinations and were accepted into the military service. It is noteworthy that these States constitute about one-quarter of all and are mostly located in the Middle West. Next come the States from which 65 to 69 per cent of the applicants were accepted, and these are indicated by light cross hatching. This group is about equal in numbers with the first, and most of them are contiguous to the first group either on the east or west. The third group makes still poorer records. Here from 60 to 64 per cent of the young men passed the tests. The States are indicated by heavy diagonal bars. Most of them were in the South and far West. Finally, there is a group of States, including, like each of the other groups, about one-quarter of all, and indicated on the map in solid black. Here are the States from which 50 to 59 per cent of the candidates were accepted. They are found in the Northeast and the far West, especially in those portions of the West which have in recent years become popular as health resorts and so have attracted large numbers of physically subnormal people. In general, it is noteworthy that the best records are made by those States that are agricultural rather than industrial and where the numbers of recently arrived immigrants are not large. Conversely, most of the States making low records are preeminently manufacturing States and also have in their populations large numbers of recently arrived immigrants.

Further analysis of the records of physical examinations shows that the country boys made better records than those from the cities; the white registrants better than the colored; and native-born better records than those of alien birth. These differences are so considerable that 100,000 country boys would furnish for the military service 4,790 more soldiers than would an equal number of city boys. Similarly, 100,000 whites would furnish 1,240 more soldiers than would an equal number of colored. Finally, 100,000 native-born would yield 3,500 more soldiers than would a like number of foreign-born. The importance of these differences may be appreciated by noting that 3,500 men is equivalent to an infantry regiment at full war strength.

200,000 OFFICERS.

About 200,000 commissioned officers were required for the Army. Of this number, less than 9,000 were in the Federal service at the beginning of the war. Of these, 5,791 were Regulars and 3,199 were officers of the National Guard in the Federal service. Diagram 6 shows with approximate accuracy the sources of the commissioned strength of the Army.

The figures show that of every six officers one had had previous military training in the Regular Army, the National Guard, or the ranks. Three received the training for their commissions in the officers' training camps. The other two went from civilian life into the Army with little or no military training. In this last group the majority were physicians, a few of them were ministers, and most of the rest were men of special business or technical equipment, who were taken into the supply services or staff corps.

THE SHARE OF EACH STATE.

A summary of the results attained is shown in diagram 7 on page 23, which gives the number of soldiers (not including officers) furnished by each State. The bars are proportionate in length to the total number of men furnished, whether by volunteering in the Regular Army, coming in through the National Guard, or being inducted through the draft.

SUMMARY.

1. The number of men serving in the armed forces of the Nation during the war was 4,800,000, of whom 4,000,000 served in the Army.

2. In the War with Germany the United States raised twice as many men as did the Northern States in the Civil War, but only half as many in proportion to the population.

3. The British sent more men to France in their first year of war than we did in our first year, but it took England three years to

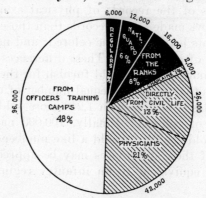

Diagram 6.—Sources of the commissioned personnel.

reach a strength of 2,000,000 men in France, and the United States accomplished it in one-half of that time.

4. Of every 100 men who served, 10 were National Guardsmen, 13 were Regulars, and 77 were in the National Army (or would have been if the services had not been consolidated).

5. Of the 54,000,000 males in the population, 26,000,000 were registered in the draft or were already in service.

6. In the physical examinations the States of the Middle West made the best showing. Country boys did better than city boys; whites better than colored; and native born better than foreign born.

7. In this war twice as many men were recruited as in the Civil War and at one-twentieth of the recruiting cost.

8. There were 200,000 Army officers. Of every six officers, one had previous military training with troops, three were graduates of officers' training camps, and two came directly from civil life.

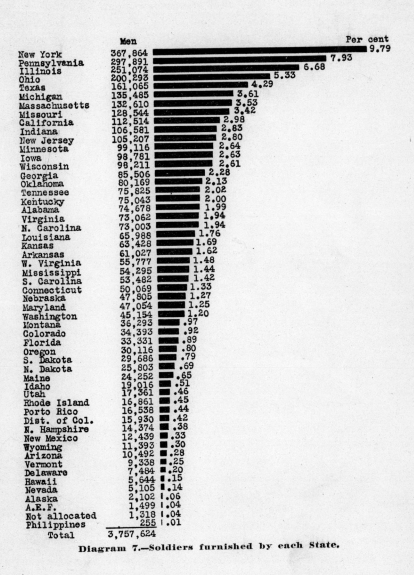

	Men		Per cent
			9.79
New York	367,864		7.93
Pennsylvania	297,891		6.68
Illinois	251,074		5.33
Ohio	200,293		4.29
Texas	161,065		
Michigan	135,485		3.61
Massachusetts	132,610		3.53
Missouri	128,544		3.42
California	112,514		2.98
Indiana	106,581		2.83
New Jersey	105,207		2.80
Minnesota	99,116		2.64
Iowa	98,781		2.63
Wisconsin	98,211		2.61
Georgia	85,506		2.28
Oklahoma	80,169		2.13
Tennessee	75,825		2.02
Kentucky	75,043		2.00
Alabama	74,678		1.99
Virginia	73,062		1.94
N. Carolina	73,003		1.94
Louisiana	65,988		1.76
Kansas	63,428		1.69
Arkansas	61,027		1.62
W. Virginia	55,777		1.48
Mississippi	54,295		1.44
S. Carolina	53,482		1.42
Connecticut	50,069		1.33
Nebraska	47,805		1.27
Maryland	47,054		1.25
Washington	45,154		1.20
Montana	36,293		.97
Colorado	34,393		.92
Florida	33,331		.89
Oregon	30,116		.80
S. Dakota	29,686		.79
N. Dakota	25,803		.69
Maine	24,252		.65
Idaho	19,016		.51
Utah	17,361		.46
Rhode Island	16,861		.45
Porto Rico	16,538		.44
Dist. of Col.	15,930		.42
N. Hampshire	14,374		.38
New Mexico	12,439		.33
Wyoming	11,393		.30
Arizona	10,492		.28
Vermont	9,338		.25
Delaware	7,484		.20
Hawaii	5,644		.15
Nevada	5,105		.14
Alaska	2,102		.06
A.E.F.	1,499		.04
Not allocated	1,318		.04
Philippines	255		.01
Total	3,757,624		

Diagram 7.—Soldiers furnished by each State.

Chapter II.

SIX MONTHS OF TRAINING.

THE AVERAGE MAN.

The average American soldier who went to France received six months of training in this country before he sailed. After he landed overseas he had two months of training before entering the battle line. The part of the battle line that he entered was in a quiet sector and here he remained one month before going into an active sector and taking part in hard fighting.

The experiences of thousands of soldiers differ widely from the typical figures just presented, but a careful study of the training data of nearly 1,400,000 men who actually fought in France gives the average results shown above. In summary they are that the average American soldier who fought in France had six months of training here, two months overseas before entering the line, and one month in a quiet sector before going into battle.

THE DIVISIONS.

The Infantry soldier was trained in the division, which was our typical combat unit. In the American Army it was composed of about 1,000 officers and 27,000 men. Training and sorting organizations of about 10,000 men, known as depot brigades, were also utilized, but as far as possible the new recruits were put almost immediately into the divisions which were the organizations in which they would go into action.

Before the signing of the armistice there were trained and sent overseas 42 American divisions. The training of 12 more was well advanced, and there were 4 others that were being organized. The plans on which the Army was acting called for 80 divisions overseas before July, 1919, and 100 divisions by the end of that year.

Table 2 lists the divisions that were organized and trained before the signing of the armistice. The different columns show the number by which each division was designated, the camp where it was trained, and the States from which its members came at the time of organization. In many cases the original composition was afterwards greatly changed by bringing in replacements to make up for losses.

25

TABLE 2.—*Place of organization of divisions and sources by States.*

Division.	Camp.	States from which drawn.
Regulars:		
1st	France	Regulars.
2nd	France	Regulars.
3rd	Greene, N. C.	Regulars.
4th	Greene, N. C.	Regulars.
5th	Logan, Tex.	Regulars.
6th	McClellan, Ala.	Regulars.
7th	MacArthur, Tex.	Regulars.
8th	Fremont, Calif.	Regulars.
9th	Sheridan, Ala.	Regulars.
10th	Funston, Kans.	Regulars.
11th	Meade, Md.	Regulars.
12th	Devens, Mass.	Regulars.
13th	Lewis, Wash.	Regulars.
14th	Custer, Mich.	Regulars.
15th	Logan, Tex.	Regulars.
16th	Kearny, Calif.	Regulars.
17th	Beauregard, La.	Regulars.
18th	Travis, Tex.	Regulars.
19th	Dodge, Iowa.	Regulars.
20th	Sevier, S. C.	Regulars.
National Guard:		
26th	Devens, Mass.	New England.
27th	Wadsworth, S. C.	New York.
28th	Hancock, Ga.	Pennsylvania.
29th	McClellan, Ala.	New Jersey, Virginia, Maryland, District of Columbia.
30th	Sevier, S. C.	Tennessee, North Carolina, South Carolina.
31st	Wheeler, Ga.	Georgia, Alabama, Florida.
32nd	MacArthur, Tex.	Michigan, Wisconsin.
33rd	Logan, Tex.	Illinois.
34th	Cody, N. Mex.	Nebraska, Iowa, S. Dakota, Minnesota, N. Dakota.
35th	Doniphan, Okla.	Missouri, Kansas.
36th	Bowie, Tex.	Texas, Oklahoma.
37th	Sheridan, Ohio.	Ohio.
38th	Shelby, Miss.	Indiana, Kentucky, West Virginia.
39th	Beauregard, La.	Arkansas, Mississippi, Louisiana.
40th	Kearny, Calif.	California, Colorado, Utah, Arizona, New Mexico.
41st	Fremont, Calif.	Various States.
42nd	Mills, N. Y.	Various States.
National Army:		
76th	Devens, Mass.	New England, New York.
77th	Upton, N. Y.	New York City.
78th	Dix, N. J.	Western New York, New Jersey, Delaware.
79th	Meade, Md.	Northeastern Pennsylvania, Maryland, District of Columbia.
80th	Lee, Va.	Virginia, West Virginia, Western Pennsylvania.
81st	Jackson, S. C.	North Carolina, South Carolina, Florida, Porto Rico.
82nd	Gordon, Ga.	Georgia, Alabama, Tennessee.
83rd	Sherman, Ohio.	Ohio, Western Pennsylvania.
84th	Zachary Taylor, Ky.	Kentucky, Indiana, Southern Illinois.
85th	Custer, Mich.	Michigan, Eastern Wisconsin.
86th	Grant, Ill.	Chicago, Northern Illinois.
87th	Pike, Ark.	Arkansas, Louisiana, Mississippi, Southern Alabama.
88th	Dodge, Iowa.	North Dakota, Minnesota, Iowa, Western Illinois.
89th	Funston, Kans.	Kansas, Missouri, South Dakota, Nebraska.
90th	Travis, Tex.	Texas, Oklahoma.
91st	Lewis, Wash.	Alaska, Washington, Oregon, California, Idaho, Nebraska, Montana, Wyoming, Utah.
92nd	Funston, Kans.	Colored, various States.
93rd	Stuart, Va.	Colored, various States.

The divisions are in three groups. The Regular Army divisions, numbered from 1 to 20, were originally made up from Regular Army units plus voluntary enlistments and selective-service men. The National Guard divisions, numbered from 26 to 42, came in largely from the militia of the several States. The National Army divisions, numbered from 76 to 92, were made up almost wholly of men called in by the selective-service law. As an aid to memory it may be helpful to note that the Regular Army divisions were numbered below 25, the National Guard divisions from 25 to 50, and the National Army divisions between 50 and 100.

All the divisions shown in the table reached France except the 12 Regular Army divisions numbered from 9 to 20. The divisions being organized at the time of the signing of the armistice were numbered 95, 96, 97, and 100.

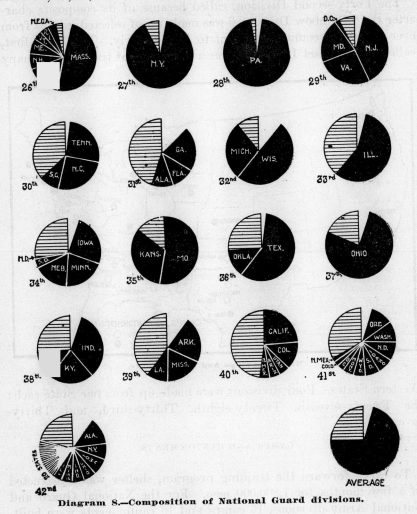

Diagram 8.—Composition of National Guard divisions.

The sources of the National Guard divisions are shown in diagram 8. The black portion of each circle shows the part of each division drawn from the National Guard; the shaded portion represents troops drawn from the National Army and other sources; and the unfilled gap in each circle represents the number of troops that the division was short of its authorized strength when it sailed.

Reference to the lower right-hand circle in the diagram shows that the average composition of these National Guard divisions was one made up of about two-thirds State troops and one-third other troops. This illustrates the noteworthy fact that one tendency of the methods of divisional organization was to produce composite divisions made up of men from most varied sources.

The Forty-second Division, called because of its composite character the "Rainbow Division," was made up of selected groups from over the entire country and sent to France early. The Forty-first, called the "Sunset Division," was a composite of troops from many

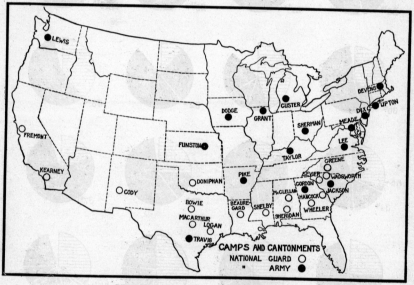

Map 2 —Camps and cantonments.

Western States. Four divisions were made up from one State each: the Twenty-seventh, Twenty-eighth, Thirty-third, and Thirty-seventh.

CAMPS AND CANTONMENTS.

To carry forward the training program, shelter was constructed in a few months for 1,800,000 men. For the National Guard and National Army divisions, 16 camps and 16 cantonments were built. National Guard units being organized rapidly during the summer of 1917 were put under canvas in camps throughout the South. The cantonments were largely in the North for the National Army called in the fall of 1917. The location of these 32 training areas is shown in map 2 on this page.

One National Guard division, the Rainbow, required no training field, for it was assembled directly at Camp Mills for early transportation to France. Two National Army divisions, the Ninety-second (colored) and the Ninety-third (colored), were trained in separate units at various camps. The headquarters of the Ninety-second were at Camp Funston and those of the Ninety-third at Camp Stuart. The remaining 16 National Guard and 16 National Army divisions began their training in the camps and cantonments in the summer and fall of 1917.

The building of the cantonments was authorized in May, 1917; the last site was secured on July 6, and on September 4 accommodations were ready for 430,000 men. This capacity was shortly increased to 770,000, an average capacity per cantonment of 48,000. Construction of the camps went forward at the same rapid pace. Although tents were provided for housing the soldiers, a considerable number of wooden buildings were necessary, as well as water supply, sewerage, electric light, and roadway construction. The capacity of the camps reached 684,000, giving a total camp and cantonment capacity of nearly a million and a half.

The Regular Army divisions were trained in part at one or another of these 32 centers, in part as separate units at various Army posts.

Troops had to be accommodated at many other points besides the 32 camps and cantonments. There were schools for training men for special services, such as the Artillery, Aviation, Engineer Corps, Chemical Warfare, Tank Corps, Quartermaster Corps. There were proving grounds and testing fields. There were also large embarkation camps at New York and Newport News. For these purposes housing was constructed with a capacity for more than 300,000 men.

INSTRUCTORS FOR TRAINING 4,000,000 MEN.

In the American Army there is one officer for each 20 men. This means that 200,000 officers were required for the army of 4,000,000 men. But when war was declared there were only 6,000 officers in the Regular Army. The National Guard divisions were fortunately able to furnish most of their own officers. After this source of supply had been exhausted, however, it was still necessary to secure some 180,000 officers elsewhere.

The officers' training camp was the instrumentality that really solved the problem of securing the commissioned personnel of the American Army. The successful precedents of the Plattsburg camps were followed. Candidates for the camps were selected after rigid tests as to physical and mental qualifications, many Reserve Corps officers being included. Three months of intensive training put the prospective officers through all the tasks required of the enlisted man and the duties of the platoon and company commander. This type of training camp furnished the Army with nearly half its total number of officers and more than two-thirds of those for line service. Diagrams 9 and 10 show some details about the graduates of these training camps.

Diagram 9 shows the ranks of the commissions granted. By far the largest number of graduates were given the grade of second lieu-

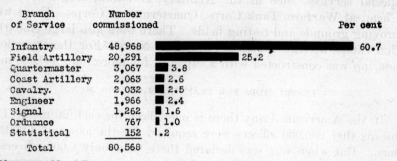

Rank	Number commissioned		Per cent
Colonels	2		
Lieutenant Colonels	1		
Majors	294	.4	
Captains	5,429	6.7	
First Lieutenants	12,397	15.4	
Second Lieutenants	62,445		77.5
Total	80,568		

Diagram 9.—Officers commissioned from training camps, by ranks.

tenant, but exceptional ability, coupled with previous military training, was singled out in the first series of camps for more advanced commissions.

Diagram 10 shows the numbers of officers commissioned in each branch of the service. Infantry and Artillery absorbed seven-eighths of the graduates with the Infantry taking more than twice as many as the Artillery. The total of 80,568 is not the grand total of gradu-

Branch of Service	Number commissioned		Per cent
Infantry	48,968		60.7
Field Artillery	20,291	25.2	
Quartermaster	3,067	3.8	
Coast Artillery	2,063	2.6	
Cavalry.	2,032	2.5	
Engineer	1,966	2.4	
Signal	1,262	1.6	
Ordnance	767	1.0	
Statistical	152	.2	
Total	80,568		

Diagram 10.—Officers commissioned from training camps, by services.

ates of officers' training schools but only of schools training officers for line duty. After the close of the second series of schools in November, 1917, it was found desirable for various staff corps and departments to conduct separate specialized schools for training their officers and many commissions were granted in these staff schools in addition to those shown in the diagram. The Quartermaster, Engineer, Signal, Ordnance, and Statistical officers shown in diagram 10 were all graduated from the first two series of schools.

FRENCH AND BRITISH INSTRUCTORS.

Shortly after the first of the new camps were established France and England sent to the United States some of their ablest officers who had seen service on the western front to bring to our training approved methods developed in the war.   These instructors were not

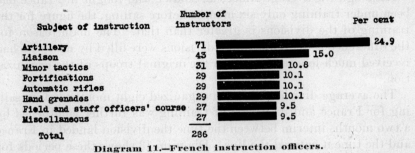

Subject of instruction	Number of instructors	Per cent
Artillery	71	24.9
Liaison	43	15.0
Minor tactics	31	10.8
Fortifications	29	10.1
Automatic rifles	29	10.1
Hand grenades	29	10.1
Field and staff officers' course	27	9.5
Miscellaneous	27	9.5
Total	286	

Diagram 11.—French instruction officers.

numerous but the aid they rendered was of the first importance. Diagrams 11 and 12 show how the subjects of instruction were divided among them.

Diagram 11 gives the information for the French officers, who were 286 in number.   Their major specialties were Artillery and staff work.   Corresponding details for the English officers are shown

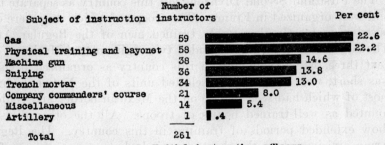

Subject of instruction	Number of instructors	Per cent
Gas	59	22.6
Physical training and bayonet	58	22.2
Machine gun	38	14.6
Sniping	36	13.8
Trench mortar	34	13.0
Company commanders' course	21	8.0
Miscellaneous	14	5.4
Artillery	1	.4
Total	261	

Diagram 12.—British instruction officers.

in diagram 12.   These military specialists were 261 in number and much of their effort was devoted to instruction in gas and physical training.

In addition to the officers shown, the British also detailed 226 non-commissioned officers as instructors, who were assigned to different subjects in about the same ratio as the officers.   These groups of foreign instructors attached to training schools, divisions, and other units, rendered service out of all proportion to their number.   They were a significant contribution to our training program.

LENGTH OF TRAINING.

Of the 42 American divisions which reached France, 36 were organized in the summer and early autumn of 1917. The other 6 were organized as divisions by January, 1918, but had been in training as separate units months before that time.

Although the average American soldier who fought in France had been under training only six months before sailing, the figure for the training of the divisions is greater than that. The main reason for the difference is that gaps in the divisions were filled by men who had received much less training than the original troops of the organization.

The average division had been organized eight months before sailing for France and its period of training was further lengthened by a two months interim between the time the division landed in France and the time it entered the line. Diagram 13 shows these periods for each of the 42 divisions. Each division is represented by a horizontal bar. The hollow part shows the period from organization to arrival of headquarters in France; the lightly hatched part, the time in France before entering line; the heavily hatched part, the time between entering the line for the first time and engaging in combat in an active sector; and the solid portion the length of service as an active battle organization.

The First and Second Divisions left this country as separate units and were organized in France. The troops of which they were composed were mostly thoroughly trained men of the Regular Army. The Second Division also included two regiments of Marines. The next three, while their stay in this country as organized divisions was short, were composed of selected units of the National Guard, most of which had seen service on the Mexican border and could be counted as well-trained bodies of troops. All the other divisions show extended periods of training in this country. The Regular Army divisions show the shortest periods, but were made up of the most experienced soldiers.

It is noticeable that all but two of the National Guard and National Army divisions were organized in August and September, 1917. The two exceptions to the rule were the Twenty-ninth, whose records show that it started the process of reorganization a few days ahead of schedule, and the Ninety-second (colored) Division which for a number of months trained in separte units at a number of different camps.

The conclusion to be drawn from the diagram would seem to be that the average American division entered battle only after 10 or

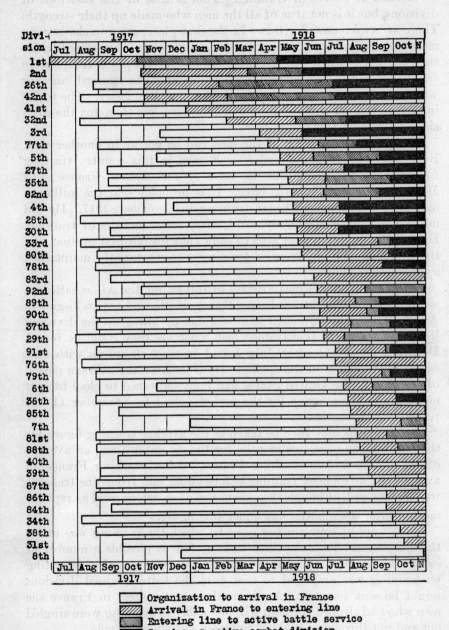

Diagram 13.—Time from organization of divisions to entering line.

11 months of thorough training. This is true of the skeletons of divisions, but it is not true of all the men who made up their strength. There are two reason for this. In the first place, some weeks or even months usually elapsed from the time a division was organized to the time when it reached full strength. In the second place, troops were frequently taken from one division to bring up to strength another which was sailing, or to be sent overseas to replace losses. The training of individual enlisted men was therefore less than for the divisions as organizations.

The length of training of the men can be got at in another way. By September, 1917, we had 500,000 men in this country training for overseas duty. We did not have 500,000 men in France until May, 1918, or eight months later. It is probable that the millionth man who went overseas began training in December, 1917. He did not reach France until July, 1918, after seven months of training. Evidence of this character goes to show that for our first million men the standard of seven months' training was consistently maintained as an average figure.

In June with the German drives in full swing, the Allies called on us to continue the extraordinary transportation of troops begun in April. The early movement had been met by filling up the divisions that sailed with the best trained men wherever they could be found. Divisions embarked after July 1 had to meet shortages with men called to the colors in the spring. By November the average period of training in the United States had been shortened to close to four months, and the average for the period July 1 to November 11 was probably five months.

Seven months may then be taken as the average training figure for the first million men, five months for the second million, an average of six months before reaching France. After reaching France an average of two months' training before going into front-line trenches was maintained, although the experience of divisions used as replacements in the last months was under this figure.

There were of course many cases in which the training was under these averages. To make these cases as few as possible a number of safeguards were set up. In this country a careful system of reporting on training was arranged so that only the better trained divisions might be sent forward. At the replacement centers in France the men who had slipped through without sufficient training were singled out and put through a 10 days' course in handling the rifle.

In the last months of the war, the induction of men was carried forward at top speed and every device was used for hastening training. The result fully justified the effort. Into the great Meuse-Argonne offensive we were able to throw a force of 1,200,000 men while we had many thousands of troops engaged in other parts of the line. Our training-camp officers stood up to the test; our men, with their intensive drilling in open-order fighting, which has characterized American training, routed the best of the German divisions from the Argonne Forest and the valley of the Meuse.

SUMMARY.

1. The average American soldier who fought in France had six months of training here, two months overseas before entering the line, and one month in a quiet sector before going into battle.

2. Most soldiers received their training in infantry divisions which are our typical combat units and consist of about 1,000 officers and 27,000 men.

3. Forty-two divisions were sent to France.

4. More than two-thirds of our line officers were graduates of the officers' training camps.

5. France and England sent to the United States nearly 800 specially skilled officers and noncommissioned officers who rendered most important aid as instructors in our training camps.

Chapter III.

TRANSPORTING 10,000 MEN A DAY.

SENDING THE TROOPS OVERSEAS.

During the 19 months of our participation in the war more than 2,000,000 American soldiers were carried to France. Half a million of them went over in the first 13 months and a million and a half in the last 6 months. Within a few weeks of our entrance into the war we began, at the earnest request of our cobelligerents, to ship

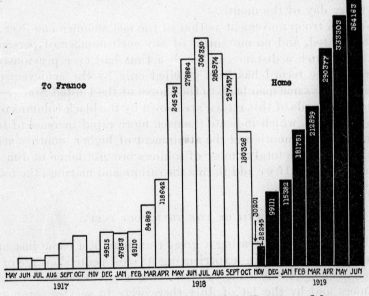

Diagram 14.—Men sailing each month to France and home.

troops overseas. At first the movement was not rapid. We had only a few American and British troop ships chartered directly from their owners. During the early winter, as the former German liners came into service, embarkations increased to a rate of nearly 50,000 per month, and by the end of 1917 had reached a total of 194,000.

The facts as to the transportation of troops to France and back to the United States are presented in diagram 14, in which the upright columns show the number carried each month.

37

Early in 1918 negotiations were entered into with the British Government by which three of its big liners and four of its smaller troop ships were definitely assigned to the service of the Army. The results of this are shown in the increased troop movement for March. It was in this month that the great German spring drive took place in Picardy, with a success that threatened to result in German victory. Every ship that could be secured was pressed into service. The aid furnished by the British was greatly increased. It was in May and the four following months that the transport miracle took place. The number of men carried in May was more than twice as great as the number for April. The June record was greater than that of May, and before the 1st of July 1,000,000 men had been embarked.

The record for July exceeded all previous monthly totals, the number of troops carried being more than 306,000. Before the end of October the second million men had sailed from our shores. During many weeks in the summer the number carried was more than 10,000 men a day, and in July the total landed averaged more than 10,000 for every day of the month.

No such troop movement as that of the last summer had ever been contemplated, and no movement of any such number of persons by water for such a distance and such a time had ever previously occurred. The record has been excelled only by the achievement in bringing the same men back to the shores of the United States. The monthly records of this return are shown by the black columns of the same diagram, which indicate the even more rapid increase of totals from month to month and the attainment of higher monthly accomplishments. The total number of soldiers brought home in June was nearly 360,000. If we add to this the sailors and marines, the total is more than 364,000.

GROWTH OF THE TRANSPORT FLEET.

The necessity for creating a great transport fleet came just at the time when the world was experiencing its most acute shortage of tonnage. The start was made by chartering a few American merchant steamers and by the 1st of July there were in service seven troop ships and six cargo ships with a total dead-weight capacity of 94,000 tons.

Diagram 15 shows how there was developed from these small beginnings a great transport fleet which aggregated by the end of 1918 three and one-quarter million dead-weight tons of shipping. The size of the fleet each month is shown by the figures in the bars of the diagram. It will be noted that each bar is divided in two parts, the portion on the left showing the dead-weight tonnage of the troop ships and that on the right the tonnage of the cargo ships.

During these same months another great American transport fleet, of which little has been said in the public press, was created with an almost equally striking rapidity. This was our cross-Channel fleet, which carried cargo and men from England to France. Its growth is pictured in the bars of diagram 16, in which the figures also represent the number of dead-weight tons from month to month. Beginning with 7,000 tons in October, 1917, this fleet consisted of more than a third of a million tons by the end of 1918. About one-fourth of the vessels were Swedish or Norwegian, while the rest were American. This service utilized large numbers of small wood

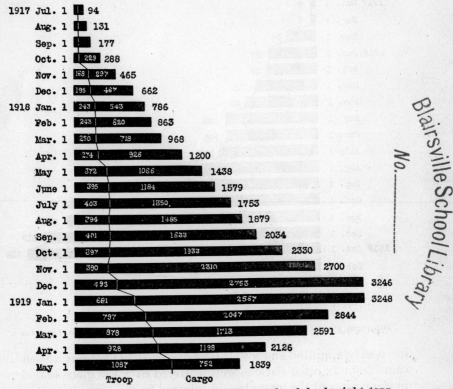

	Troop	Cargo	
1917 Jul. 1			94
Aug. 1			131
Sep. 1			177
Oct. 1	229		288
Nov. 1	168	297	465
Dec. 1	195	467	662
1918 Jan. 1	243	543	786
Feb. 1	243	620	863
Mar. 1	250	718	968
Apr. 1	274	926	1200
May 1	372	1066	1438
June 1	395	1184	1579
July 1	403	1350	1753
Aug. 1	394	1485	1879
Sep. 1	401	1633	2034
Oct. 1	397	1933	2330
Nov. 1	390	2310	2700
Dec. 1	493	2753	3246
1919 Jan. 1	681	2567	3248
Feb. 1	797	2047	2844
Mar. 1	878	1713	2591
Apr. 1	928	1198	2126
May 1	1087	752	1839

Diagram 15.—The trans-Atlantic fleet in thousands of deadweight tons.

and steel vessels built by the Emergency Fleet Corporation at the yards of the Great Lakes and along the coast.

WHERE THE SHIPS CAME FROM.

In building up our trans-Atlantic and Channel fleets every possible source of tonnage had to be called on for every ship that could be secured. The first great increment was the seized German vessels, which came into service during the fall of 1917.   The taking over of Dutch steamers in the spring of 1918 and the chartering of Scandinavian and Japanese tonnage accounted for great increases in the cargo fleet. Map 3, on page 41, shows the amounts of tonnage that were secured for our Army fleet from the different countries of the world.

The most ample credit must be given to the Emergency Fleet Corporation, which turned over nearly a million tons of new ships, and to the Shipping Control Committee, which stripped bare of all suitable vessels our import and export trades and turned over for Army

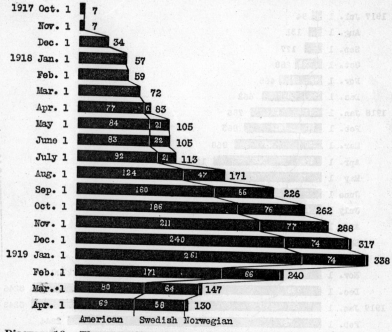

Diagram 16.—The cross-Channel fleet, in thousands of deadweight tons.

use nearly a million and a half tons of ships.   The Army vessels also came from 12 other nations well scattered over the globe and shown in the figures of the map already referred to.

EMBARKATION AND DEBARKATION.

Most of the troops who sailed for France left from New York. Half of them landed in England and the other half landed in France.   Most of those who landed in England went directly to Liverpool and most of those who landed in France went to Brest. While these statements are valid generalizations, they fall short in showing what happened in detail.   The principal facts of the eastward troop movement are shown in map 4, on page 42.

Troops left America from 10 ports, as shown in the little table in the left of the map. In this table the several ports of Hoboken, New York, and Brooklyn have all been included in one, and the same thing is true of the different ports at Hampton Roads, which have been shown under the heading of Newport News.

While 10 American ports were used, including 4 in Canada, more than three-quarters of all the men went from New York. The ports of arrival are given in the tables on the right of the map, which show that the ports of debarkation in Europe were even more numerous than those of embarkation in America.

HELP FROM THE ALLIES.

Credit for the troop movement must be shared with the Allies, and with the British in particular, since approximately half of the

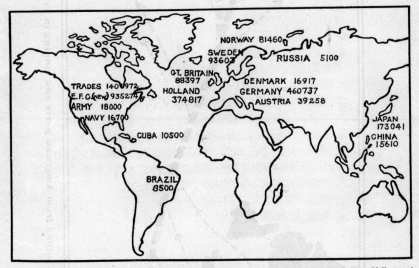

Map 3.—Deadweight tons of American Army shipping secured from different countries.

troops were carried in their ships. This is shown by the figures of diagram 17.

Among every hundred men who went over, 49 went in British ships, 45 in American ships, 3 in those of Italy, 2 in French, and 1 in Russian shipping under English control. Part of the explanation for the large numbers of troops carried in American ships is to be found from the fact that under the pressure of the critical situation on the western front, ways were found to increase the loading of our own transports by as much as 50 per cent. In addition, our transports exceeded those of the Allies in the speed of their turnarounds. The facts as to the average number of days taken by the ships

GLASGOW 45000
MANCHESTER 4000
LIVERPOOL 844000
BRISTOL PORTS 11000
FALMOUTH 1000
PLYMOUTH 1000
SOUTHAMPTON 57000
LONDON 62000
102.5000

LE HAVRE 13000
BREST 791000
ST NAZAIRE 198003
LA PALLICE 4000
BORDEAUX 50000
MARSEILLE 1000
1057000

To Italy 2,000

QUEBEC 11000
MONTREAL 34000
ST. JOHNS 1000
HALIFAX 5000
PORTLAND 6000
BOSTON 46000
NEW YORK 1656000
PHILA. 35000
BALTIMORE 4000
NEWPORT NEWS 288000
2086000

Map 4.—Troops sailing from American ports and landing in France and England.

to go to Europe, discharge their cargo and troops, come back, take
on another load, and start for France once more, are shown in
Diagram 18.

The cycle of operations is termed "a turnaround," and it is
not complete until the vessel has taken its load over, discharged it,
returned, reloaded, and actually started on another trip. When our
ships began operations in the spring of 1917 the average turnaround for the troop ships was 52 days, and that for the cargo
ships 66 days. These performances were improved during the
summer months, but became very much longer during the exceptionally cold winter of 1917. During the spring, summer, and fall
of 1918 the performances of both cargo and troop ships became

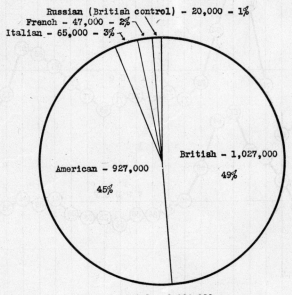

Diagram 17.—American troops carried by ships of each nation.

standardized at about 70 days for cargo ships and 35 days for troop
ships.

In noting these facts, as presented in the figures of the diagram,
it is to be borne in mind that the figures refer to the lengths of
the turnarounds of all the ships sailing from American ports in
one month. Thus the high figure of 109 days for the cargo ships
means that 109 days was the average time required for all the
cargo ships leaving American ports in November to complete their
turnarounds and start on their next trips. These vessels made
their trips in the exceptionally cold months of December, January,
and February.

The fastest ships have averaged under 30 days. During the spring and summer of 1918 the *Leviathan*, the former *Vaterland*, has averaged less than 27 days, as has the *Mount Vernon*, the former *Kronprinzessen Cecelie*. These turnarounds, made under the embarrassment of convoy, are much quicker than anything attained in commercial operation. During the summer the *Leviathan* has transported troops at the rate of over 400 a day, and so has landed

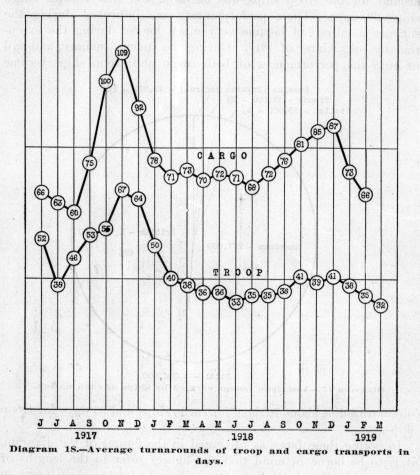

Diagram 18.—Average turnarounds of troop and cargo transports in days.

the equivalent of a German division in France each month. Two American ships, the *Great Northern* and *Northern Pacific*, have averaged 25 and 26 days, respectively, and have each made turnarounds in 19 days.

CARGO MOVEMENT.

The first shipment of cargo to support the forces abroad was made in June, 1917, and amounted to 16,000 tons. After the first two months the shipments grew rapidly and steadily until they were in excess of 800,000 tons in the last month of the war. These facts are shown in diagram 19.

The shipment of cargo differs from that of troops in that it was done almost entirely by American ships. Less than 5 per cent of the cargo carried was transported in allied bottoms. The great bulk of the cargo was carried in the cargo ships shown in diagram 15 on page 39. Relatively small amounts were carried in the troop ships.

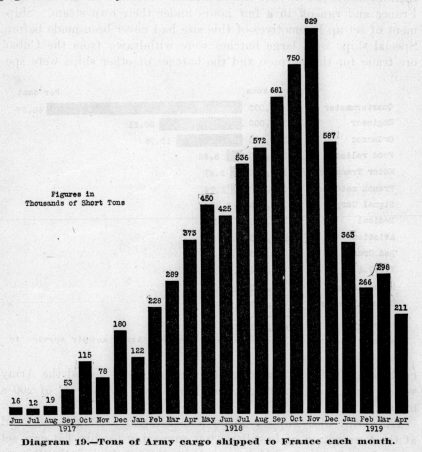

Figures in
Thousands of Short Tons

Jun Jul Aug Sep Oct Nov Dec Jan Feb Mar Apr May Jun Jul Aug Sep Oct Nov Dec Jan Feb Mar Apr
1917   1918   1919

Diagram 19.—Tons of Army cargo shipped to France each month.

After the signing of the armistice every ship was withdrawn from the service as soon as it could be spared and put back into trades or the carrying of food for relief work in Europe. By April the total cargo fleet was only a third as large as it had been five months before.

The cargo carried for the American Army consisted of thousands of different articles of the most varied sort. Something of this variety is revealed by diagram 20, which shows the number of short tons carried for each of the Army supply services and for the special agencies. Nearly one-half of all consisted of quartermaster material, largely composed of food and clothing. The next largest elements were engineering and ordnance supplies. All together, from our entrance into the war through April, 1919, the Army shipped from this side of the Atlantic nearly seven and a half million tons of cargo.

Included in the cargo shipment were 1,791 consolidation locomotives of the 100-ton type. Of these, 650 were shipped set up on their own wheels, so that they could be unloaded on the tracks in France and run off in a few hours under their own steam. Shipment of set-up locomotives of this size had never been made before. Special ships with large hatches were withdrawn from the Cuban ore trade for the purpose and the hatches of other ships were spe-

	Short tons		Per cent
Quartermaster	3,606,000		48.39
Engineer	1,506,000		20.21
Ordnance	1,189,000		15.96
Food relief	285,000		3.82
Motor Transport	214,000		2.87
French material	208,000		2.79
Signal Corps	121,000		1.62
Medical	111,000		1.49
Aviation	61,000		.82
Red Cross	60,000		.81
Y.M.C.A.	45,000		.60
Miscellaneous	35,000		.47
Chemical Warfare	11,000		.15
Total	7,452,000		

Diagram 20.—Tons of cargo shipped for each Army supply service to April 30, 1919.

cially lengthened, so that when the armistice was signed the Army was prepared to ship these set-up locomotives at the rate of 200 a month.

The Army also shipped 26,994 standard-gauge freight cars, and at the termination of hostilities was preparing to ship flat cars set up and ready to run. Motor trucks to the number of 47,018 went forward, and when fighting ceased were being shipped at the rate of 10,000 a month. Rails and fittings for the reinforcing of French railways and for the construction of our own lines of communications aggregated 423,000 tons. In addition to the tons of cargo mentioned above the Army shipped 68,694 horses and mules, and at the cessation of hostilities was shipping them at the rate of 20,000 a month. The increase in the shipment of cargo from the United States was consistently maintained from the start of the war, and at its cessation was undergoing marked acceleration.

Aside from the cargo shipped across the Atlantic, Gen. Pershing imported large amounts from European sources, the chief item being coal from England. In October he brought into France by means of his cross-Channel fleet a total of 275,000 tons of coal and other commodities.

LOSSES AT SEA.

During the whole period of active hostilities the Army lost at sea only 200,000 deadweight tons of transports. Of this total 142,000 tons were sunk by torpedoes. No American troop transport was

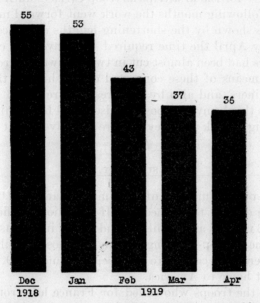

Diagram 21.—Average days required to convert cargo ships to troop transports.

lost on its eastward voyage. For this splendid record the Navy, which armed, manned, and convoyed the troop transports, deserves the highest commendation.

RETURN OF TROOPS.

In diagram 14, on page 37, figures are presented showing the number of troops brought back to the United States from France each month since the signing of the armistice. The figures mount even more rapidly and reach higher totals than those of the eastward journeys.

As soon as the armistice was signed preparations were made for returning the troops to the United States in the shortest possible time. This was rendered difficult by the fact that for the eastward movement we had relied largely on the British, who carried approximately half of all the troops. After the signing of the armistice the British needed these ships for the return of their own colonial troops, to Canada, Australia, and South Africa.

This situation was met by the Army Transport Service, which immediately began the conversion of our large cargo ships into troop-carrying vessels. Diagram 21 shows the number of days that were required to convert cargo ships into troop-carrying transports. The upright columns of the diagram are proportional to the number of days required. The ships upon which work was begun in December were not ready for the first trips as troop carriers until 55 days later. During the following months the work went forward more and more rapidly, as is shown by the shortening lengths of the columns in the diagram. By April the time required for converting cargo ships to troop carriers had been almost cut in two and was approximately one month. By means of these converted cargo ships, by the assignment of German liners, and also by the great aid rendered by the Navy, which put at the Army's disposal cruisers and battleships, the Army is being brought back home even more rapidly than it was taken to France.

SUMMARY.

1. During our 19 months of war more than 2,000,000 American soldiers were carried to France. Half a million of these went over in the first 13 months and a million and a half in the last 6 months.

2. The highest troop-carrying records are those of July, 1918, when 306,000 soldiers were carried to Europe, and June, 1919, when 364,000 were brought home to America.

3. Most of the troops who sailed for France left from New York. Half of them landed in England and the other half landed in France.

4. Among every 100 Americans who went over 49 went in British ships, 45 in American ships, 3 in Italian, 2 in French, and 1 in Russian shipping under English control.

5. Our cargo ships averaged one complete trip every 70 days and our troop ships one complete trip every 35 days.

6. The cargo fleet was almost exclusively American. It reached the size of 2,700,000 deadweight tons and carried to Europe about 7,500,000 tons of cargo.

7. The greatest troop-carrier among all the ships has been the *Leviathan*, which landed 12,000 men, or the equivalent of a German division, in France every month.

8. The fastest transports have been the *Great Northern* and the *Northern Pacific*, which have made complete turnarounds, taken on new troops, and started back again in 19 days.

Chapter IV.

FOOD, CLOTHING, AND EQUIPMENT.

THE PROBLEM OF PURCHASE.

In the spring of 1917 there were in the United States some 4,000,-
000 young men who were about to become soldiers, although they
little suspected the fact. Before they entered the Army, as well as
after they were in it, these men consumed such ordinary necessities
of life as food, coats, trousers, socks, shoes, and blankets.

These simple facts lead directly to the mistaken conclusion that the
problem of supplying the necessities of life for the soldiers in the
Army was the comparatively simple one of diverting into the camps
substantially the same amounts of food and clothing as these young
men would have used in their homes if there had been no war.

These men constituted about one twenty-fifth of the population
of the country and undoubtedly consumed before the war more than
one twenty-fifth of the food and clothing used in the United States.
But after every possible allowance has been made for the requirements of youth and the wastefulness of war, the figures of Army
purchases still present surprising contrasts with those of civilian
use in normal times.

Some of these contrasts are shown in diagram 22, which compares
total American production of blankets, wool gloves, wool socks, and
men's shoes in 1914, as given in the census of manufactures, with
Army purchases of the same articles in 1918.

The first two columns of the diagram relate to blankets. They
show that the Army purchases in 1918 were two and one-quarter
times as great as the entire American production in 1914. To put it
another way, the figures mean that the blankets bought in one year
for the use of 4,000,000 or 5,000,000 soldiers would have been sufficient
to make good the actual normal consumption of blankets by 100,000,-
000 American civilians for two and a quarter years. From the data
of the other columns of the same diagram similar, if not equally surprising, comparisons may be made.

The reasons for the enormous figures of Army purchases are not far
to seek. In the first place, men who went to camp received complete
equipment of new articles, whereas ordinary production in peace time

goes mainly to replace articles that have been worn out. In the second place, the supplies required for an army increase in proportion to the distance that separates the army from its home base. In the third place, the consumption in action is three or four times the peace rate.

The stream of supplies going forward to an army may be likened to the water delivered against a fire by an old-fashioned bucket brigade. For every pailful thrown on the fire there must be many that have been taken from the source of supply and are on the way. As

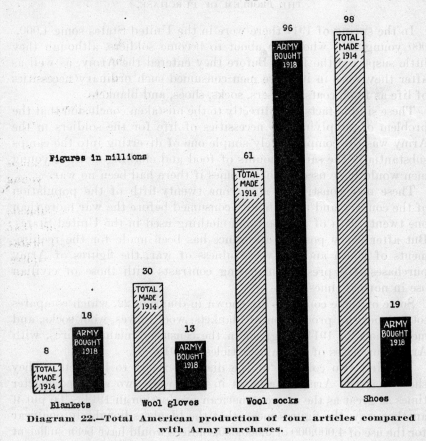

Diagram 22.—Total American production of four articles compared with Army purchases.

the distance from the source increases this supply in transit constantly grows. When an army is 3,000 or 4,000 miles from its sources of supply the amounts of supplies in reserve and in transit are enormous as compared with the quantities actually consumed each month.

The rule generally followed for clothing was that there should be for each man at the front a three months' reserve in France, another two or three months' reserve in the United States, and a third three months' supply continuously in transit. Wool coats, for example, last about three months in active service. Hence for every coat on a man's back at the front there had to be a coat in reserve in France, a coat in transit, and a coat in reserve in the United States. For every man at the front four coats were needed, and needed as soon as he went overseas. Two million men overseas required something like 8,000,000 coats, and required them immediately.

The same thing was true for other supplies and munitions. The need for reserves and the time required for transportation called for the supply of enormous quantities and called for it at once. The immediate needs for each man sent forward were in fact far in excess of the later requirements. For munitions difficult to manufacture, such as artillery and ammunition, the problem presented by this necessity for reserves and large amounts in transit, in addition to the actual equipment of troops, was almost insuperable. The initial need is so great in a situation of this character that it can only be met in one of two ways; either by having the initial equipment available at the outbreak of war, or by immediately securing such an enormous productive capacity that it is larger than is required for maintaining the establishment later.

In supplying food and clothing and other articles which are matters of common commercial production, the problem was not as difficult as with ordnance, but the large needs for initial equipment did put an enormous strain upon the industries concerned. A list of the total deliveries during the war of some of the common articles of clothing shows the size of the task. They are given in Table 3. The cost of the articles listed was more than $1,000,000,000.

TABLE 3.—*Clothing delivered to the Army April 6, 1917, to May 31, 1918.*

Articles.	Total delivered.	Articles.	Total delivered.
Wool stockings..............pairs..	131,800,000	Blankets.............................	21,700,000
Undershirts........................	85,000,000	Wool breeches......................	21,700,000
Underdrawers......................	83,600,000	Wool coats.........................	13,900,000
Shoes......................pairs..	30,700,000	Overcoats..........................	8,300,000
Flannel shirts......................	26,500,000		

All these garments could be made in ordinary commercial factories, but their quantity was so enormous that at a number of times during the war it was feared that the demand would run ahead of the supply. When the troop movement was speeded up in the spring of 1918 the margin on woolen clothing was dangerously narrow. To secure these and other articles in sufficient quantity it was found necessary in many cases for the Army to take control of all stages of the manufacturing process, from assembling the raw material to inspecting the finished product. For many months preceding the armistice the War Department was owner of all the wool in the country. From September, 1918, to June, 1919, if the troop movement had continued, Army needs were estimated at 246,000,000 pounds of clean wool, while the amount allotted to civilian needs was only 15,000,000 pounds. The British Army had in a similar way some years before taken control of the English wool supply in order to meet army and navy needs. Their requirements were, however, less than ours, to the extent that they did not need such a large reserve in France and practically none in transit. Their requirements per man for equipment were for this reason about two-thirds as great as ours.

Something the same story might be told for about 30,000 kinds of commercial articles which the Army purchased. Purchases included food, forage, hardware, coal, furniture, wagons, motor trucks, lumber, locomotives, cars, machinery, medical instruments, hand tools, machine tools. In one way or another the Army at war drew upon almost every one of the 344 industries recognized by the United States Census. In some cases readjustments of machinery for a slightly modified product were necessary. In many an improved product was demanded. In practically all an enormous production was required. In the cases of some articles all the difficulties of quantity production were combined with the problems of making something not before manufactured. Typical instances are the 5,400,000 gas masks and the 2,728,000 steel helmets produced before the end of November, 1918.

MACHINERY OF DISTRIBUTION.

For those supplies that were to a certain degree articles of commercial manufacture, the problem of distribution was fully as difficult as procurement. For production, machinery already in existence could be utilized; for distribution, a new organization was necessary. In this country the problem was not hard for there were ample railway facilities; an abundance of motor transportation could be requisitioned if necessary; and the troops were near the sources. In France, a complete new organization was necessary whose main duty it was to distribute munitions and supplies. It was called the Services of Supply, the S. O. S., and had its headquarters at Tours. It was an army behind the Army. On the day the armistice was signed, there were reporting to the commanding general of the Services of Supply, 386,000 soldiers besides 31,000 German prisoners, and thousands of civilian laborers furnished by the Allies. At the same time there were in the zone of the armies 160,000 noncombatant troops, the majority of whom were keeping in operation the lines of distribution of supplies to the troops at the front. The proportion of noncombatants in the American Army never fell below 28 per cent. In the British Army it often ran higher. Even when there was the greatest pressure for men at the front, the work back of the lines took roughly one man out of every three.

Distributing supplies to the American forces in France was in the first place a problem of ports, second a problem of railroads, third

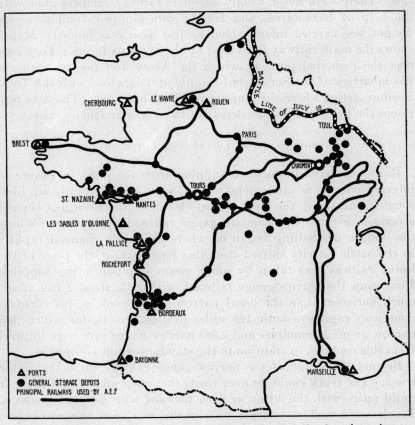

Map 5.—Seaports, storage points, and supply lines of the American Army in France.

a problem of motor and norse-drawn transportaion, and fourth a problem of storage.

The ports and railroads of France were crowded with war traffic and fallen into disrepair. It was not necessary to build new ports, but American engineers added 17 new berths, together with warehouses and dock equipment. It was not necessary to build new railroads, for France already had a railway net denser per square mile than that of the United States, but it was desirable to increase the carrying capacity by nearly 1,000 miles of new trackage, and by switching facilities at crucial points, by new repair shops and roundhouses, and by new rolling stock. These things were done by the Engineers. The problems were not wholly solved. There were never enough docks to prevent some loss of time by vessels waiting to dock, but the capacity for handling American cargo was tripled from 10,000 tons per day in the spring of 1918 to 30,000 tons by November 11 and the waiting time of ships was shorter than in commercial practice. There were never wholly adequate railway facilities, but with the help of locomotives and freight cars shipped from this side freight was carried inland about as fast as it was landed. Map 5 shows the main railway lines used by the overseas forces. They connect the principal ports at which the Army fleet docked with the headquarters of the Services of Supply at Tours and with the Toul-Verdun sector, where the American armies operated. The dots represent the principal storage depots of the transportation service.

NARROW-GAUGE RAILWAYS AND MOTOR TRUCKS.

Railroads carried American supplies from the ports in France to intermediate or advance depots. As map 5 shows, railroad lines roughly paralleled the front. Spurs led up to the front, but beyond a certain distance the standard-gauge railroad did not go. Where the danger of shelling began or where the needs changed rapidly as the battle activity shifted from this front to that, the place of the heavy railway was taken by other means of distributing supplies. First came the narrow-gauge railroad, with rails about 2 feet apart, much narrower than the usual narrow-gauge road in this country. American engineers built 125 miles of these roads, for which 406 narrow-gauge locomotives and 2,385 narrow-gauge cars were shipped from this country, in addition to the standard-gauge equipment.

Beyond the range of the narrow-gauge railway came the motor truck. The truck could go over roads that were under shell fire. It could retire with the Army or push forward with advancing troops. Trucks were used on a larger scale in this war than was ever before thought possible. The American Infantry division on the march with the trucks, wagons, and ambulances of its supply, ammunition, and sanitary trains stretches for a distance of 30 miles along the road. The 650 trucks which the tables of organization of the division provide are a large factor in this train. The need for trucks increased moreover during the latter months of the war as trench warfare gave place to a war of movement. As the forces moved forward on the offensive away from their railway bases, more and more trucks were demanded.

The Army overseas never had all the trucks it needed during the period of hostilities. Diagram 23 shows how the supply, month by month, measured up to the numbers called for in the tables of organization. The dash line shows the truck tonnage needed and the heavy line the amount available.

The supply was least adequate during the last four months of the war, when the shipment of trucks fell behind the accelerated troop movement. The difficulty was almost entirely a shortage of ships. At practically all times there were quantities of trucks at the ports of embarkation, but trucks take enormous amounts of cargo space on ships. It is slow and difficult work to load them, and time after time embarkation officials were forced to leave the trucks standing

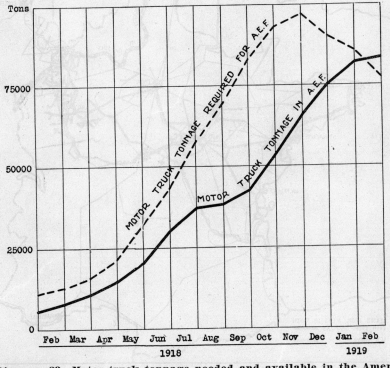

Diagram 23.—Motor-truck tonnage needed and available in the American Expeditionary Forces.

at the ports and load their ships rapidly with supplies needed still more urgently overseas. In October and November more ships were pulled out of the trades and the trucks were shipped even at the expense of other essential supplies. The shipment kept pace with the troop movement, but the initial shortage could not be overcome until February. The number of trucks sent overseas prior to the armistice was 40,000 and of these 33,000 had been received in France. The trucks ranged in size from three-quarters of a ton to 5 tons.

Beyond the range of the motor truck the horse and wagon were the means of supply distribution. Here again the American armies made an inadequate equipment do the work that was required. The shipment of animals overseas was discontinued early in 1918 on the information that horses could be purchased overseas. Then in the fall when every ton of shipping was precious, the supply of foreign horses proved inadequate and 23 of the best of the Army's cargo

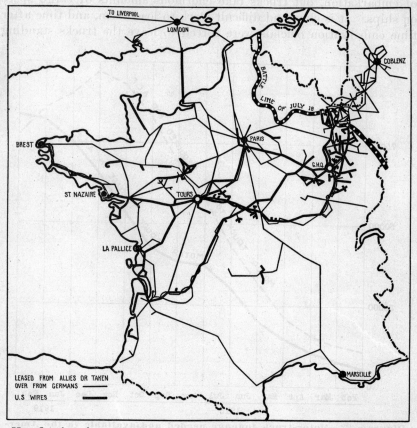

Map 6.—American telephone and telegraph lines in France, England, and Germany.

vessels had to be converted to animal transports. About 500 horses and mules were embarked in September and 17,000 in October. The shipments could not, however, be started soon enough to prevent a shortage. A horse uses as much ship space as 10 tons of cargo, but in the latter months the need for animals was so great that this sacrifice was made.

In general, it may be said that the Army overseas never had enough means of transportation. It may also be said that they had very large quantities and that they produced remarkable results with the supply they had.

47,000 TELEGRAMS A DAY.

In order to operate the transportation of supplies in France, a new system of communication had to be set up; so the Signal Corps strung its wires over nearly every part of France. This is shown in map 6.

The heavy lines indicate telephone and telegraph lines wholly constructed by Americans or wires strung on French poles. The light lines are wires leased from the French or taken over from the Germans. Trunk lines led from all the principal ports to Paris, to Tours, and to general headquarters (G. H. Q.) back of the American battle areas. The lines running to Coblenz for the army of

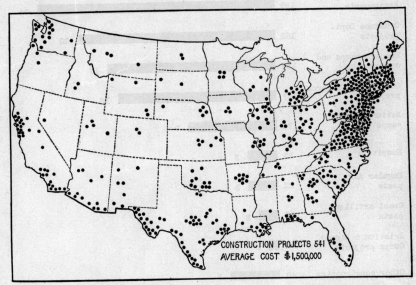

CONSTRUCTION PROJECTS 541
AVERAGE COST $1,500,000

Map 7.—Construction projects of the Army in the United States.

occupation were taken over from the Germans. At the time of the signing of the armistice the Signal Corps was operating 282 telephone exchanges and 133 complete telegraph stations. The telephone lines numbered 14,956, reaching 8,959 stations. More than 100,000 miles of wire had been strung. The peak load of operation reached was 47,555 telegrams a day, averaging 60 words each.

CONSTRUCTION IN THE UNITED STATES.

To build factories and storage warehouses for supplies, as well as housing for troops, 200,000 workmen in the United States were kept continuously occupied for the period of the war.. The force of workers on this single activity was larger than the total strength of both southern and northern armies in the Battle of Gettysburg. The types of construction included cement piers and warehouses, equipment for proving grounds, plants for making powder and explosives, repair shops, power plants, roads, and housing for troops. Building was required in every State of the Union, as shown in map 7. Each dot represents a construction project.

The region of greatest activity was the Northeast, at once the most densely populated section and the center of munitions production.

Housing constructed had a capacity of 1,800,000 men, or more than the entire population of Philadelphia. The operations of the

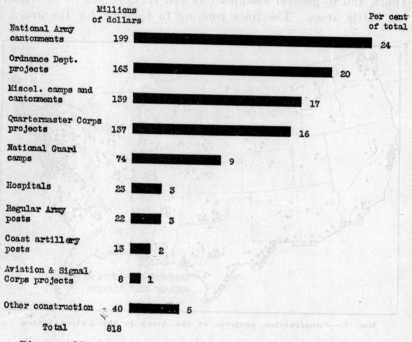

	Millions of dollars		Per cent of total
National Army cantonments	199		24
Ordnance Dept. projects	163		20
Miscel. camps and cantonments	139		17
Quartermaster Corps projects	137		16
National Guard camps	74		9
Hospitals	23		3
Regular Army posts	22		3
Coast artillery posts	13		2
Aviation & Signal Corps projects	8		1
Other construction	40		5
Total	818		

Diagram 24.—Costs of construction projects in the United States.

Construction Division constituted what was probably the largest contracting business ever handled in one office.

The total expenditures in this enterprise to November 11, 1918, were, in round numbers, $800,000,000, or about twice the cost of the Panama Canal. The per cent of the total which was allotted to various purposes is shown in diagram 24. The largest single item is the cost of National Army cantonments which was nearly one-quarter of the total. Ordnance Department projects, including the building of enormous powder, high-explosive, and loading plants, come second.

The costs of construction were probably higher than they would have been for slower work. The outstanding feature of the accomplishment was its rapidity. Each of the cantonments was completed in substantially 90 days. It was this speed that made it possible to get the draft army under training before the winter of 1917 set in and made it available just in time for the critical action of the summer of 1918.

CONSTRUCTION IN THE A. E. F.

The conduct of the war in France necessitated a construction program comparable in magnitude and number of projects with that in the United States. Less new building was required for shelter and

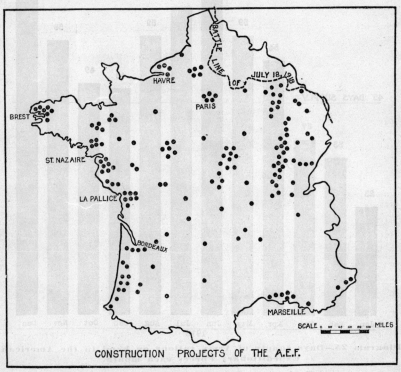

CONSTRUCTION PROJECTS OF THE A.E.F.

Map 8.—Construction projects of the Army in France.

for the manufacture of munitions, but more for the development of port and railroad facilities and for the repair and operation of the complicated equipment of a modern army.

The storage space constructed in France was more than nine-tenths as large as the amount built at home. Hospital capacity constructed in France was twice the new capacity at home.

All construction work in France was performed by the Corps of Engineers under the Services of Supply. The labor force consisted largely of American soldiers and German prisoners, although French and English civilians and Chinese coolies were used wherever available. To economize tonnage materials were obtained in Europe as far as possible, sometimes at high prices. The Engineer Corps ran its own quarries and its own logging camps and sawmills. Only such materials as could not be obtained abroad—chiefly machinery and steel products—were purchased in the United States.

Up to the signing of the armistice construction projects had been undertaken by the Corps of Engineers to the number of 831. Their

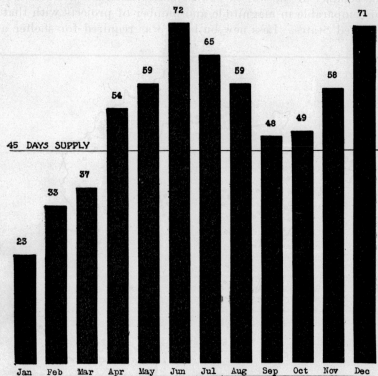

Diagram 25.—Days supply of Army rations on hand in the American Expeditionary Forces each month.

distribution over France is shown in map 8, in which every dot represents a place at which one or sometimes several projects were undertaken. The A. E. F. left its trail in the shape of more or less permanent improvements over the greater part of France. The projects cluster most thickly around the ports used by American forces and the American area on the southern end of the battle line.

FOOD AND CLOTHING AT THE FRONT.

The real test of the efficiency of the supply service comes when an army engages in battle. Measured by that test the work of feeding, clothing, and equipping the American Army was well done for, in the main, the expeditionary forces received what they needed. Within the limits of this report no account can be given in detail of how fully the supplies received overseas met the needs of the troops. A few typical and fundamentally important items only can be selected. Food and clothing are the most essential.

At no time was there a shortage of food in the expeditionary forces. Soldiers sometimes went hungry in this as in all other wars, but the condition was local and temporary. It occurred because of transportation difficulties during periods of active fighting or rapid movement when the units outran their rolling kitchens. The stocks of food on hand in depots in France were always adequate. This is illustrated in diagram 25. The columns show the stocks of food in depots on the first of each month in terms of how many days they would last the American forces then in France.

During the winter and spring of 1918 the amounts on hand rose steadily. On May 1, about the time when American troops were entering active fighting for the first time, they were well over the 45-day line, which was considered the required reserve during the latter months of the war. For a time efforts were made to build up a 90-day supply in order that the overseas forces might continue to operate for some months, even if the lines of supply across the ocean were cut. As the menace of the submarine becomes less acute, and as the need of ship tonnage for other supplies became more pressing, the required reserve was cut to 45 days. It will be seen from the diagram that at no time during the period of active operations did the reserve fall below this line.

In the matter of clothing also, the supply services rose to the emergency of combat.

There were periods in the history of many individual units when needed supplies could not be immediately obtained but, as in the case of food, the difficulty was one of local transportation.

The records of the Quartermaster show that during the six months of hard fighting, from June to November, the enlisted man in the A. E. F. received on the average:

Slicker and overcoat, every 5 months.

Blanket, flannel shirt, and breeches, every 2 months.

Coat, every 79 days.

Shoes and puttees, every 51 days.

Drawers and undershirt, every 34 days.

Woolen socks, every 23 days.

SUMMARY.

1. The problems of feeding and clothing the Army were difficult because of the immense quantities involved rather than because of the difficulty of manufacturing the articles needed.

2. Requirements for some kinds of clothing for the Army were more than twice as great as the prewar total American production of the same articles.

3. To secure the articles needed for the Army the Government had to commandeer all the wool and some other staple articles in the United States and control production through all its stages.

4. The distribution of supplies in the expeditionary forces required the creation of an organization called the Services of Supply, to which one-fourth of all the troops who went overseas were assigned.

5. American Engineers built in France 17 new ship berths, 1,000 miles of standard-gauge track, and 125 miles of narrow-gauge track.

6. The Signal Corps strung in France 100,000 miles of telephone and telegraph wire.

7. Prior to the armistice 40,000 trucks were shipped to the forces in France.

8. Construction projects in the United States cost twice as much as the Panama Canal, and construction overseas was on nearly as large a scale.

9. The Army in France always had enough food and clothing.

Chapter V.

SPRINGFIELDS, ENFIELDS, AND BROWNINGS.

RIFLES.

During the years immediately preceding our entrance into the war there was much discussion within the War Department, as well as in the country at large, of the need for increased military preparedness. Reference to the department reports for 1914, 1915, and 1916 shows that what was then considered as the best military and civilian opinion was agreed that the army that would have to be called into the field in any large emergency was one of 500,000 men.

In these reports attention was called to the fact that while our available resources in trained men, in airplanes, and in machine guns were entirely inadequate, our reserve stocks of rifles and small-arms ammunition were sufficient for even a larger Army than the half million suggested.

On the outbreak of hostilities there were on hand nearly 600,000 Springfield rifles of the model of 1903. This arm is probably the best Infantry rifle in use in any army, and the number on hand was sufficient for the initial equipment of an army of about 1,000,000 men. What no one foresaw was that we should be called upon to equip an army of nearly 4,000,000 men in addition to furnishing rifles for the use of the Navy.

The emergency was met in several different ways. The available Springfields were used to equip the Regular Army and National Guard divisions that were first organized. In addition to these rifles we also had in stock some 200,000 Krag-Jörgensen rifles that had been stored for an emergency and were in sufficiently good condition to be used for training purposes. In addition, efforts were made to speed up the manufacture of new Springfields.

It was soon found, however, that manufacturing difficulties would make it impossible to increase the output of Springfields to much beyond 1,000 per day, which was clearly insufficient. At this juncture decision was reached to undertake the manufacture of an entirely new rifle to meet the deficiency.

Fortunately, there were in this country several plants which were just completing large orders for the Enfield rifle for the British Government. A new rifle—the model 1917—was accordingly designed. This rifle resembled the British Enfield sufficiently so that the plants equipped for Enfield production could be rapidly converted to its manufacture, but it was chambered to use the same ammunition as is used in the Springfield and in the machine guns and automatic rifles of American manufacture.

Diagram 26 shows the number of Springfields and Enfields accepted to the end of each month from the beginning of the war up

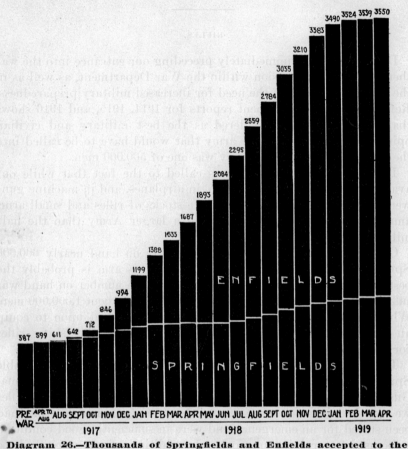

Diagram 26.—Thousands of Springfields and Enfields accepted to the end of each month.

to the end of April, 1919. The figures include the prewar stock of Springfields.

Beginning with slightly less than 600,000 Springfields at the outbreak of the war, the total at the end of the war had increased to nearly 900,000. The Enfields first came into production in August, 1917. After their manufacture had actually begun the output increased rapidly until it totaled at the end of the war, in November, 1918, nearly 2,300,000.

During the entire period the production of spare parts for the Springfield rifles was continued at an increased rate. The first divisions sent to France were equipped with this rifle. It is a fact that about half the rifle ammunition used against the enemy by United States troops was shot from Springfield rifles. The test of battle use has upheld the high reputation of the Springfield, and has demonstrated that the American Enfield is also a weapon of superior quality. The American troops were armed with rifles that were superior in accuracy and rapidity of fire to those used by either their enemies or the Allies.

MACHINE GUNS.

The use of machine guns on a large scale is a development of the European war. This is demonstrated by the records of every army. In the case of the American forces the figures are particularly impressive. In 1912 Congress sanctioned the allowance of the War Department of four machine guns per regiment. In 1919, as a result of the experience of the war, the new Army plans provide for an equipment of 336 machine guns per regiment. The second allowance is 84 times as great as the one made seven years earlier.

In the annual report of the Secretary of War for 1916, transmitted in the fall of that year, attention was called to the efforts then being made to place our Army on a satisfactory footing with respect to machine guns. The report says:

Perhaps no invention has more profoundly modified the art of war than the machine gun. In the European War this arm has been brought into very great prominence. * * * When the Congress at the last session appropriated $12,000,000 for the procurement of machine guns, it seemed important, for obvious reasons, to free the air of the various controversies and to set at rest in as final a fashion as possible the conflicting claims of makers and inventors. A board was therefore created. * * * A preliminary report has been made by this board, selecting the Vickers-Maxim type for heavy machine guns, recommending the purchase of a large supply of them, and fixing a date in May at which time exhaustive tests to determine the relative excellence of various types of light machine guns are to be made.

In accordance with these recommendations, 4,000 Vickers machine guns were ordered in December, 1916. By the end of the next year 2,031 of them had been delivered. In further accord with the recommendations of the board, careful tests were held in May, 1917, of various types of heavy machine guns, and also of light machine guns, which have come to be known as automatic rifles. Rapidity of fire, freedom from stoppage and breakage, accuracy, weight, ease of manufacture, and other factors were all carefully examined.

The Vickers gun justified the good opinion previously formed of it, but it was clear that it could not be put on a quantity-production basis because of technical difficulties in manufacture. Fortunately, a new gun well adapted to quantity production was presented for trial. This gun, the heavy Browning, performed satisfactorily in all respects and was adopted as the ultimate standard heavy machine gun. The light Browning, designed by the same expert, was easily in the lead as an automatic rifle, weighing only 15 pounds. The Lewis gun, too heavy for satisfactory use as an automatic rifle and not capable of the long-sustained fire necessary in a heavy gun, was very well suited, with slight modification, for use as a so-called flexible gun on aircraft. A small number (2,500) of these guns were ordered for training purposes for ground use, but the bulk of the possible production of this gun was assigned to aircraft purposes. In addition to the flexible type, airplanes require also a synchronized gun; that is, a gun whose time of firing is so adjusted that the shots pass between the propeller blades. The Vickers gun had been used successfully for this purpose in Europe and the call was insistent for their diversion to this use, both for our own planes and for those of the French. After many trials and adjustments, however, the Marlin gun, a development of the old Colt, was adapted to this purpose, releasing part of the early production of Vickers guns for ground use. A subsequent development was the design of a modified form of the heavy Browning for aircraft use as a synchronized gun.

Production of all the types mentioned was pressed and the advantages of preparedness illustrated. The placing of the order for 4,000 Vickers in 1916 enabled 12 of our early divisions to receive that weapon as their heavy machine gun. The thorough trial given in May, much earlier than would have been possible except for previous plans, made possible a selection of suitable types for every purpose and the completion of the first light Brownings in February, 1918, and the first heavy Brownings in April of the same year.

The remarkable rise in the rate of production is shown by months in diagram 27. The rise was broken only in September, the month of the influenza epidemic.

The earliest needs of our troops in France were met by French Hotchkiss machine guns and Chauchat automatic rifles. A little later, divisions going over were provided with Vickers heavy guns and Chauchat automatic rifles. After July 1, divisions embarking were equipped with light and heavy Brownings. Both Browning guns met with immediate success and with the approval of foreign officers as well as with that of our own.

Although the light and the heavy Browning guns were brought into production in February and April of 1918, they were not used in battle until September. This was not because of any shortage of supply in the later summer months but because of a deliberate and most significant judgment on the part of Gen. Pershing. After

careful tests of the new weapons had been made in Europe the
American commander in chief decided that the two new Brownings
were so greatly superior to any machine guns in use by any of the
armies on either side that the wisest course would be to wait until
several divisions could be equipped with them and a plentiful future
supply assured before using them in battle at all.

What he feared was that if the first of the guns to reach the expeditionary forces were used in battle there would always be some

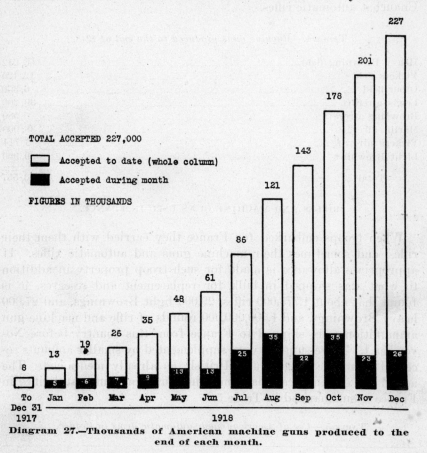

Diagram 27.—Thousands of American machine guns produced to the
end of each month.

chance that one might be captured by the Germans. If this should
happen it was possible that with their quick recognition of the importance of any military improvement and the demonstrated German
industrial capacity for quantity production, they might begin the
immediate manufacture of German Brownings. In this event the
advantage of the possession of large numbers of greatly improved
types of machine guns and automatic rifles would be partly lost to
the American forces.

For these reasons the Brownings were not used in combat until they were used in large numbers in the Meuse-Argonne battle. There they amply justified the faith of the American commander and the Ordnance Department in their superior qualities.

The total number of machine guns of American manufacture produced to the end of 1918 is shown in Table 4. In addition there were secured from the French and British 5,300 heavy machine guns, of which nearly all were French Hotchkiss guns, and 34,000 French Chauchat automatic rifles.

TABLE 4.—*Machine guns produced to the end of 1918.*

Heavy Browning field	56,612
Vickers field	12,125
Other field	6,366
Lewis aircraft	39,200
Browning aircraft	580
Marlin aircraft	38,000
Vickers aircraft	3,714
Light Browning	69,960
Total	226,557

RIFLES AND MACHINE GUNS USED IN FRANCE.

When troops embarked for France they carried with them their rifles, and sometimes their machine guns and automatic rifles. If appropriate allowance is made for such troop property in addition to what was shipped in bulk for replacement and reserves, it is found that about 1,775,000 rifles, 29,000 light Brownings, and 27,000 heavy Brownings, and 1,500,000,000 rounds of rifle and machine-gun ammunition were shipped to France from this country before November 1. These supplies were supplemented by smaller amounts received from the French and British, as already mentioned. The actual use of American-made machine guns and automatic rifles in France is summarized in Table 5.

TABLE 5.—*Use of American-made automatic arms in France.*

	Used at the front.	Total, including training.
Light Browning	4,608	17,664
Heavy Browning	1,168	3,528
Vickers ground gun	2,340	2,860
Lewis aircraft	1,393	3,930
Marlin aircraft	1,220	3,084
Vickers aircraft	1,320	1,625

PISTOLS AND REVOLVERS.

From the beginning of the war the call for pistols was insistent. In this case the American Army was fortunate in having in the Browning-Colt a weapon already in production and more effective than the corresponding weapon used by any other army. But while there never was any question as to the quality of the pistol, there was much trouble in securing them in numbers adequate to meet the demands. To help meet the situation a revolver was designed using the same ammunition, and placed in production in October, 1917. As a result the troops in France who were likely to require them for close combat were supplied with one or the other of these weapons so far as possible, but full equipment was never secured.

SMALL-ARMS AMMUNITION.

A sufficient supply of small-arms ammunition has always been available to provide for troops in service. The complication due to the use of machine guns and automatic rifles of French caliber has been successfully met. To meet the special needs of the Air Service and of antiaircraft defense, new types of ammunition have been designed and produced, the purposes of which are indicated by their names—armor piercing, tracer, and incendiary. Before the end of the war American production of small arms ammunition amounted to approximately 3,500,000,000 rounds, of which 1,800,000,000 were shipped overseas. In addition, 200,000,000 rounds were secured from the French and British.

ARMS AND THE MEN.

Diagram 28 is an attempt to answer in graphic form the question "To what degree did the different elements of our troop program and our small-arms program move forward in company front?" The upper heavy black line represents the number of men in the American Army from month to month. The lower black line represents similarly the strength of the Army in France.

On the same scale are drawn four other lines indicating widely fluctuating quantities for the different months. The lowest of these represents the size of army that could have been equipped, according to the tables of organization, with the number of pistols and revolvers actually on hand each month. The diagram shows that we never had nearly enough of these weapons to equip fully our entire Army, and only during part of the months of the war were there enough for the full equipment of the troops in France even if all the pistols and revolvers had been there and issued.

The line for automatic rifles shows an adequate supply for all troops only in the last two months of the war. That for machine guns shows inadequate supplies up to July and then so enormous a

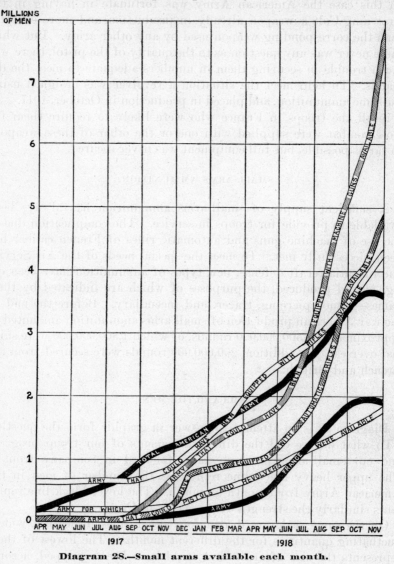

Diagram 28.—Small arms available each month.

production as to be sufficient before the end of the war for an army of nearly 8,000,000 men. The line for rifles shows relatively close agreement during the entire period. There was an initial surplus, then a deficit for six months, and after that a consistent surplus.

In the cases of automatic rifles, machine guns, and rifles there was always a supply on hand in excess of what would have been required for the equipment of the expeditionary forces alone.

In making the computations for all these comparisons an appropriate allowance has been made in every case for reserves, wastage, and time lost in transit. The curves represent as nearly as it has been possible to make them the actual balance each month between the number of men and the total equipment available. They can not, of course, take into account any shortages that may have resulted in specific localities through failures in distribution.

Only the Springfield and Enfield rifles are included in the computation of available rifles, although hundreds of thousands of Krag-Jörgensen and Russian rifles and some Canadian Ross rifles were used for training purposes.

The rapid rise of the lines representing the men that could have been equipped with machine guns and automatic rifles in the later months is due to the heavy production of Brownings. In fact, this production was one of the striking features of our war effort. It would have resulted, if the fighting had been prolonged, in a greatly increased volume of fire on the part of the American troops.

PREPARING FOR THE CAMPAIGN OF 1919.

At this point it is appropriate to comment on the fact that there are many articles of munitions in which American production reached great amounts by the fall of 1918 but which were not used in large quantities at the front because the armistice was signed before big supplies of them reached France. In the main, these munitions are articles of ordnance and aviation equipment, involving such technical difficulties of manufacture that their production could not be improvised or even greatly abbreviated in time.

As the production figures are scrutinized in retrospect, and it is realized that many millions of dollars were spent on army equipment that was never used at the front, it seems fair to question whether prudent foresight could not have avoided some of this expense.

Perhaps the best answer to the question is to be found in the record of a conference that took place in the little French town of Trois Fontaines on October 4, 1918, between Marshal Foch and the American Secretary of War.

In that conference the allied commander in chief made final arrangements with the American Secretary as to the shipment of American troops and munitions in great numbers during the fall and winter preparatory for the campaign of 1919.

This was one day before the first German peace note and 38 days before the end of the war, but Marshal Foch was then calling upon America to make her great shipments of munitions and her supreme contribution of man power for the campaign of the following year.

SUMMARY.

1. When war was declared the Army had on hand nearly 600,000 Springfield rifles. Their manufacture was continued, and the American Enfield rifle designed and put into production.

2. The total production of Springfield and Enfield rifles up to the signing of the armistice was over 2,500,000.

3. The use of machine guns on a large scale is a development of the European war. In the American Army the allowance in 1912 was four machine guns per regiment. In 1919 the new Army plans provide for an equipment of 336 guns per regiment, or eighty-four times as many.

4. The entire number of American machine guns produced to the end of 1918 was 227,000.

5. During the war the Browning automatic rifle and the Browning machine gun were developed, put into quantity production, and used in large numbers in the final battles in France.

6. The Browning machine guns are believed to be more effective than the corresponding weapons used in any other army.

7. American production of small arms ammunition amounted to approximately 3,500,000,000 rounds, of which 1,800,000,000 were shipped overseas.

8. Attention is directed to diagram 28, on page 70, comparing numbers of men under arms each month with numbers for which equipment of pistols, rifles, automatic rifles, and machine guns were available.

Chapter VI.

TWO THOUSAND GUNS ON THE FIRING LINE.

It was true of light artillery as it was of rifles, that the United States had, when war was declared, a supply on hand sufficient to equip the Army of 500,000 men that proponents of preparedness had agreed might have to take the field in the event of a large emergency. There were 900 pieces of field artillery then available. The gun on hand in largest quantities was the 3-inch fieldpiece, of which we had 544. As 50 of these are required for 1 division, this was a sufficient number to equip 11 divisions. When the emergency arrived, however, it was far larger than had been foreseen even by those who had been arguing that we needed an army several times as large as the one we then had. The initial plans called for the formation of 42 divisions, which would require 2,100 3-inch fieldpieces almost at once. In addition, these divisions would require for active operations in France a repair shop reserve, a replacement reserve, and a stream of guns in transit which would increase their initial requirements to about 3,200. To keep this army going would only require a production of about 100 guns per month, but to get it going within a reasonable length of time would have required a productive capacity of 300 or 400 guns per month, depending on how soon it was imperative for the army to be in action. The great difference between the manufacturing output necessary to get an army going quickly and that required to keep it going after it has been equipped, explains the enormous industrial disadvantage suffered by a nation which enters a war without its stocks of military supplies for initial equipment already on hand.

To meet the situation the decision was made in June, 1917, to allot our own guns to training purposes and to equip our forces in France with artillery conforming to the French and British standard calibers. The arrangement was that we should purchase from the French and British the artillery needed for our first divisions and ship to them in return equivalent amounts of steel, copper, and other raw materials so that they could either manufacture guns for us in their own factories or give us guns out of their stocks and proceed to replace them by new ones made from our materials.

The plans then formulated further provided that, with our initial requirements taken care of in this way, we should at once prepare to manufacture in our own plants artillery of these same calibers for the equipment of later divisions. In general, it may be truly said that these plans were carried through successfully along the lines originally laid down. With no serious exceptions, the guns from British and French sources were secured as needed, but our own plants were slower in producing complete units ready for use than had been hoped and planned.

In our factories the 3-inch guns of improved model which had been ordered in September, 1916, were changed in caliber to use standard French ammunition, and became known as 75 mm. guns, model 1916. The British 18-pounder then being produced in this country was similarly redesigned, and became known as the 75 mm. gun, model 1917. Work was immediately begun also on the plans for the French 75 mm. gun so as to make it possible to produce it in American factories. For this gun, however, it was necessary to develop new manufacturing capacity.

In the case of other calibers of artillery, the same means in general were taken to secure a supply. Material previously on order was adapted to meet the new conditions; capacity actually engaged on production for the French and British was utilized to as great an extent as possible, and foreign plans were adapted to American practice and new plants erected to push production. It was necessary, of course, in all this work not to interfere with American production for the Allies. Of the enormous amount of equipment made necessary by the expansion of the Army from its first strength to the contemplated force of 5,000,000 men, the artillery and artillery ammunition could be improvised with the least facility, for the necessary processes of its manufacture involved irreducible periods of time. In spite of all these handicaps, the record of actual production on United States Army orders only, is 1,642 complete units of artillery before the armistice was signed. The total production of complete units of artillery in American plants is shown by the figures of diagram 29. The data are exclusive of production for the Navy and for the Allies.

In point of fact the figures showing the number of complete units produced are somewhat unfair to the American record. The difficult problem of planning the production of the different component parts was not satisfactorily solved until about the end of the war. The result was that by the production of a single component, after the armistice was signed, hundreds of units were completed, and the totals for the months after the armistice are as large as those before October, although the work actually done in those months was very

much less. These facts are revealed by the monthly and total figures
of the diagram. Up to the end of April, 1919, the number of complete artillery units produced in American plants was more than
3,000, or equal to all those purchased abroad from the French and
British up to the signing of the armistice.

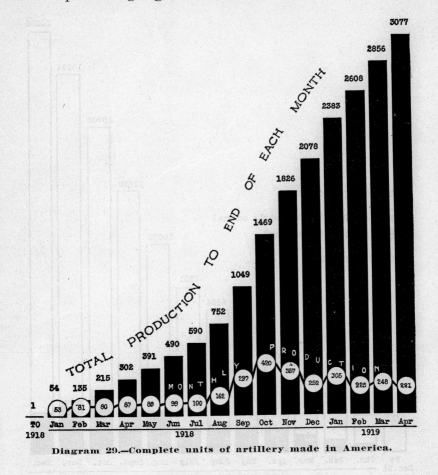

Diagram 29.—Complete units of artillery made in America.

ARTILLERY AMMUNITION.

In the magnitude of the quantities involved the Artillery ammunition program was the biggest of all. Copper, steel, high explosives,
and smokeless powder were all required by the hundreds of millions
of pounds. As no firms were prepared to manufacture complete
rounds, it was necessary for the Ordnance Department to make contracts for each component and to assume the burden of directing the
distribution of these components between manufacturers. For the
shrapnel it was possible to use the design substantially as had previ-

ously been used in this country, but the high explosive and gas shell proved more troublesome. A large supply of American shell was produced, however, before the signing of the armistice, and shipment to Europe in quantity had begun. The ammunition actually used against the enemy at the front was nearly all of French manufacture,

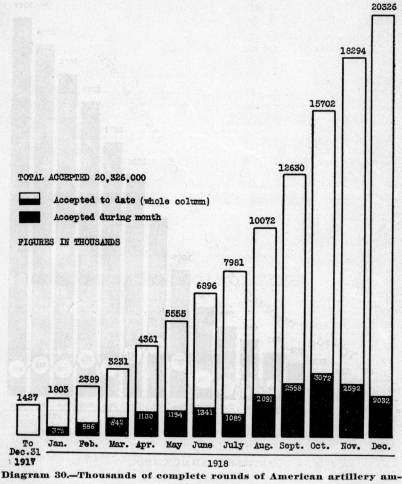

TOTAL ACCEPTED 20,326,000

■ Accepted to date (whole column)
■ Accepted during month

FIGURES IN THOUSANDS

Diagram 30.—Thousands of complete rounds of American artillery ammunition produced.

but the approaching supply from America made possible a more free use of the French and British reserves. As shown in diagram 30, our monthly production of artillery ammunition rose to over 2,000,000 complete rounds in August and over 3,000,000 rounds in October if we include United States calibers. By the end of 1918 the number of rounds of complete artillery ammunition produced in American plants was in excess of 20,000,000, as compared with 10,000,000 rounds secured from the French and British.

BRITISH AND AMERICAN ARTILLERY PRODUCTION.

One mode of measuring our accomplishments in the way of artillery production is to compare what we succeeded in producing in our own plants in the first 20 months after the declaration of war with what Great Britain produced in the first 20 months after her entry into the war. This comparison is made in diagram 31, which compares for that period of time American and British production of complete units of light and heavy artillery and rounds of light and heavy shells. Antiaircraft artillery (a small item) is not included

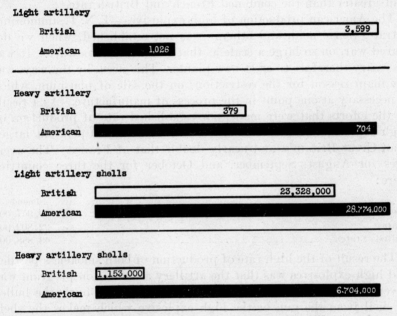

Light artillery

British — 3,599
American — 1,026

Heavy artillery

British — 379
American — 704

Light artillery shells

British — 23,328,000
American — 28,774,000

Heavy artillery shells

British — 1,153,000
American — 6,704,000

Diagram 31.—British and American production of artillery and ammunition in the first 20 months of war.

in either class. Canadian production of machined shell for Great Britain and the United States is included in each case.

In each of the comparisons of diagram 31 the bar in outline represents British production over the first 20 months, and the one in solid black the American output over the first 20 months. The figures show that the British did better than we did in the production of light artillery, but that we excelled their record in heavy artillery and in both sorts of shell production.

SMOKELESS POWDER AND HIGH EXPLOSIVES.

One of the striking contributions of the United States to the cause of the Allies was the enormous quantity of smokeless powder and high explosives produced. From April 1, 1917, to November 11, 1918, the production of smokeless powder in the United States was 632,-000,000 pounds, which was almost exactly equal to the combined production of France and Great Britain. This was not all for our own use. About half the British supply in 1917 was drawn from this country, and in 1918 over a third of the French supply was American made. This large supply was made possible in part by plants erected for the British in this country, but the American Ordnance Department also added new plants. As a result, the established rate of production in this country by the close of the war was 45 per cent greater than the combined French and British rate.

The American production of high explosives—T. N. T., ammonium nitrate, picric acid, and others—was not established, when we declared war, on so large a scale as that of smokeless powder. It was necessary therefore to erect new plants. This need, by the way, was the main reason for the restrictions on the sale of platinum, which is necessary at one point in the process of manufacture. As a result of the efforts that were made, our established rate of production of high explosives at the close of the war was over 40 per cent larger than Great Britain's, and nearly double that of France. The averages for August, September, and October for the three countries were:

	Pounds.
Great Britain	30,957,000
France	22,802,000
United States	43,888,000

The result of the high rate of production of both smokeless powder and high explosives was that the artillery ammunition program was never held up for lack of either the powder which hurls the bullet or shell from the gun or the high explosive which makes the shell effective when it reaches its destination.

TOXIC GASES.

When the clouds of chlorine suddenly enveloped the British and French lines in the Ypres salient, early in 1915, a new weapon was introduced into the war. That it was a powerful weapon is evidenced by the fact that during the year 1918 from 20 to 30 per cent of all our battle casualties were due to gas.

At the time we entered the war we had had practically no experience in manufacturing toxic gases, and no existing facilities which could be readily converted to such use. At the signing of the armistice, we were equipped to produce gas at a more rapid rate than France, England, or Germany.

In the early days of our participation in the war it was hoped that concerns engaged in chemical manufacture could be put into this new field. There were many valid objections, however, to such a plan. Many of these concerns were already crowded with war work. Entirely new equipment would have to be installed, which, in all likelihood, would be practically worthless at the close of the war. Exhaustive investigation and experimentation would mean delay in securing quantity production. The element of danger would mean

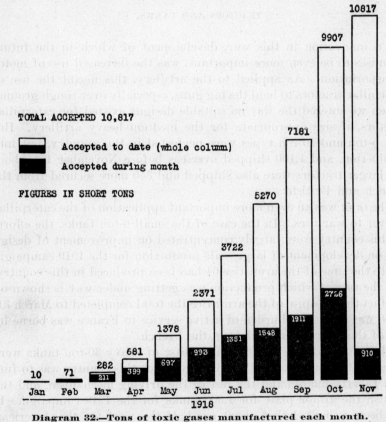

TOTAL ACCEPTED 10,817

☐ Accepted to date (whole column)

■ Accepted during month

FIGURES IN SHORT TONS

Diagram 32.—Tons of toxic gases manufactured each month.

difficulty in securing and retaining adequate labor forces. For these reasons the Government found it necessary to build its own chemical plants and to finance certain private firms. The majority of these producing plants, together with plants for filling shells with gas, were built on a tract of land in the Aberdeen Proving Ground, Md., which came to be known as the Edgewood Arsenal. The auxiliary plants were also known as Edgewood Arsenal. The columns of diagram 32 show the number of short tons of toxic gases produced in American plants each month. The increase in production was rapid and steady during 1918 and, before the armistice, more than 10,000 tons had been manufactured.

Production of gas and the capacity for filling were at all times well ahead of the supply of shell containers to be filled. In June, 1918, considerable quantities of mustard gas, chlorpicrin, and phosgene were shipped overseas for filling gas shells produced by the French. By the end of July no more French shells were available for this purpose and the surplus gas was sold to the French and British.

TRACTORS AND TANKS.

An innovation in this war, development of which in the future promises to be even more important, was the increased use of motor transportation. As applied to the artillery, this meant the use of caterpillar tractors to haul the big guns, especially over rough ground. When we entered the war no suitable designs existed for caterpillar tractors of size appropriate for the medium heavy artillery. But new 5-ton and 10-ton types were perfected in this country, put into production, and 1,100 shipped overseas before November 1. About 300 larger tractors were also shipped and 350 more secured from the French and British.

The tank was an even more important application of the caterpillar tractor to war uses. In the case of the small 6-ton tanks, the efforts of this country were largely concentrated on improvement of design and on development of large scale production for the 1919 campaign. Up to the time of the armistice 64 had been produced in this country, and the rate at which production was getting under way is shown by the fact that in spite of the armistice the total completed to March 31, 1919, was 799. The burden of active service in France was borne by 227 of these tanks received from the French.

The efforts of this country in the case of heavy 30-ton tanks were concentrated on a cooperative plan, by which this country was to furnish Liberty motors and the rest of the driving mechanism, and the British the armor plate for 1,500 tanks for the 1919 campaign. It has been estimated that about one-half the work on the American components for this project had been completed before November 11, and the work of assembly of the initial units was well under way. For immediate use in France, this country received 64 heavy tanks from the British.

OUR ARTILLERY IN FRANCE.

The most important single fact about our artillery in France is that we always had a sufficient supply of light artillery for the combat divisions that were ready for front-line service. This does not mean that when the divisions went into the battle line they always had their artillery with them, for in a number of cases they did not.

The statement does mean, however, that when divisions went into line without their artillery this was not because of lack of guns but rather because it takes much longer to train artillery troops than it does infantry and so, under the pressure of battle needs in the summer and fall of 1918, American divisions were put into line a number of times supported by French and British artillery or without artillery.

When the armistice came in November the American forces not only had a sufficient number of 75's for the 29 combat divisions, but in addition enough more for 12 other divisions.

A careful study of the battle records of all the divisions shows that if all the days in the line of all the combat divisions are added together, the total is 2,234. The records further show the number of days that each division was in line with its own artillery, with British artillery, with French, or without any.

The result of the compilation is to show that in every 100 days that our combat divisions were in line they were supported by their own artillery for 75 days, by British artillery for 5 days, by French for 1½ days, and were without artillery for 18½ days out of the 100. Of these 18½ days, however, 18 days were in quiet sectors and only one-half of one day in active sectors. There are only three records of American divisions being in an active sector without artillery support. The total of these three cases amounts to one-half of 1 per cent, or about 14 hours out of the typical 100 days just analyzed.

The most significant facts about our artillery in France are presented in summary in table 6, which takes into account only light and heavy field artillery and does not include either the small 37-mm. guns or the trench mortars.

TABLE 6.—*American artillery in France—Summary.*

Total pieces of artillery received to Nov. 11	3, 499
Number of American manufacture	477
American-made pieces used in battle	130
Artillery on firing line	2, 251
Rounds of artillery ammunition expended	8, 850, 000
Rounds of ammunition of American manufacture expended	208, 327
Rounds of American-made ammunition expended in battle	8, 400

The facts of the table can be summarized in round numbers with approximate accuracy by saying that we had in France 3,500 pieces of artillery, of which nearly 500 were made in America, and we used on the firing line 2,250 pieces, of which over 100 were made in America.

GUNS NEEDED V. GUNS AVAILABLE.

Diagram 33 shows the degree of balance which existed each month throughout the war between the men under arms and the artillery that was available for them. The number of men in the entire American Army is shown by the upper black line and the number of these who were in France is shown by the lower black line.

The upper hollow line shows the size of army that could have been fully equipped each month with the pieces of light artillery, con-

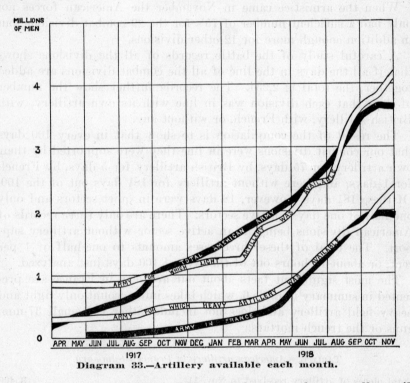

MILLIONS
OF MEN

TOTAL AMERICAN ARMY WAS AVAILABLE
ARMY FOR WHICH LIGHT ARTILLERY
ARMY FOR WHICH HEAVY ARTILLERY WAS AVAILABLE
ARMY IN FRANCE

APR MAY JUN JUL AUG SEP OCT NOV DEC JAN FEB MAR APR MAY JUN JUL AUG SEP OCT NOV
1917　　　　　　　　　　　　　1918

Diagram 33.—Artillery available each month.

sisting of 75 mm. and 3-inch field guns, that were then actually available. If the supply had been fully ample this line would run somewhat above the upper black line, to allow for an adequate reserve and for the retirement of the less satisfactory types of guns. Actually the hollow line runs below the black one from September, 1917, to September, 1918, and indicates a slight deficiency in training equipment, which was relieved in the fall of 1918 by large deliveries of the 1917 model.

In a similar way the lower black line shows for each month the size of army that could have been equipped with the proper number of pieces of heavy artillery of calibers greater than 3 inches. The measure of full equipment is based on the tables of organization adopted early in the war. These tables call for more heavy artillery for a given number of men than the French, British, or Germans actually used, and much more than had ever been thought advisable before this war.

If all our heavy field artillery had been of types suitable for use in France, we should have had enough, even on this high standard, to meet the needs of the expeditonary forces. However, as we had some types that were considered suitable only for training the shortage indicated by the diagram was a real one. The rapid rise in the latter months of the war shows that the great difficulties of manufacture of this type of material were being overcome toward the end of the war. In considering the facts presented by this diagram it is to be borne in mind that all suitable pieces of artillery are taken into account from the date they were produced or secured whether they were then located in America or in France. The comparison is between the men that we had and the guns that we had each month.

SUMMARY.

1. When war was declared the United States had sufficient light artillery to equip an army of 500,000 men, and shortly found itself confronted with the problem of preparing to equip 5,000,000 men.

2. To meet the situation it was decided in June, 1917, to allot our guns to training purposes and to equip our forces in France with artillery conforming to the French and British standard calibers.

3. It was arranged that we should purchase from the French and British the artillery needed for our first divisions and ship them in return equivalent amounts of steel, copper, and other raw materials so that they could either manufacture guns for us in their own factories or give us guns out of their stocks and replace them by new ones made from our materials.

4. Up to the end of April, 1919, the number of complete artillery units produced in American plants was more than 3,000, or equal to all those purchased from the French and British during the war.

5. The number of rounds of complete artillery ammunition produced in American plants was in excess of 20,000,000, as compared with 10,000,000 rounds secured from the French and British.

6. In the first 20 months after the declaration of war by each country the British did better than we did in the production of light artillery, and we excelled them in producing heavy artillery and both light and heavy shells.

7. So far as the Allies were concerned, the European war was in large measure fought with American powder and high explosives.

8. At the end of the war American production of smokeless powder was 45 per cent greater than the French and British production combined.

9. At the end of the war the American production of high explosives was 40 per cent greater than Great Britain's and nearly double that of France.

10. During the war America produced 10,000 tons of gas, much of which was sold to the French and British.

11. Out of every hundred days that our combat divisions were in line in France they were supported by their own artillery for 75 days, by British artillery for 5 days, and by French for 1½ days. Of the remaining 18¼ days that they were in line without artillery, 18 days were in quiet sectors, and only one-half of 1 one day in each hundred was in active sectors.

12. In round numbers, we had in France 3,500 pieces of artillery, of which nearly 500 were made in America, and we used on the firing line 2,250 pieces, of which over 100 were made in America.

Chapter VII.

AIRPLANES, MOTORS, AND BALLOONS.

PREWAR EQUIPMENT.

When war was declared in April, 1917, the United States had two aviation fields and 55 serviceable airplanes. The National Advisory Committee on Aeronautics, which had been conducting a scientific study of the problems of flight, advised that 51 of these airplanes were obsolete and the other 4 obsolescent.

This judgment was based on the operations in Mexico, which had demonstrated serious defects in the designs of American planes used there. It was well known that improved types had been developed in the European conflict, but the details of their design were carefully guarded and withheld from neutrals.

Immediately following the declaration of war, the Allied Governments, particularly the French, urged the necessity of sending 5,000 American aviators to France during the first year, if superiority in the air were to be insured. This request emphasized the need of speed. The European instructors who came over later to assist in the training work made no pretense that the 5,000 schedule was practicable. The problem was to approximate it as nearly as possible. Public expectation was greatly exaggerated, due to the general ignorance, shared by even the best informed American authorities on aviation, as to the requirements, other than simple flying ability, which this service exacts.

There were three primary requisites for bringing into existence an elementary aviation service. These were training planes, aviators, and service planes. All of them had to be created.

TRAINING.

For the task of training, as well as that of securing the necessary planes and motors, there existed in our Army no adequate organization of qualified personnel. Before the war our air service had been small, struggling, and unpopular. Aviation was restricted to unmarried officers under 30 years of age, and offered no assured future as a reward for success. It had made its greatest appeal to the younger and more daring types of line officers, and was not an organization on which a great industrial expansion could be built, or from which any large numbers of qualified instructors could be drawn.

Training for aviation divides itself into three stages—elementary, advanced, and final. Elementary training, given to all candidates alike, includes physical training, hygiene, various practical and theoretical military subjects, the study of the structure and mechanism of airplanes and engines, signaling, observation, ground gun-

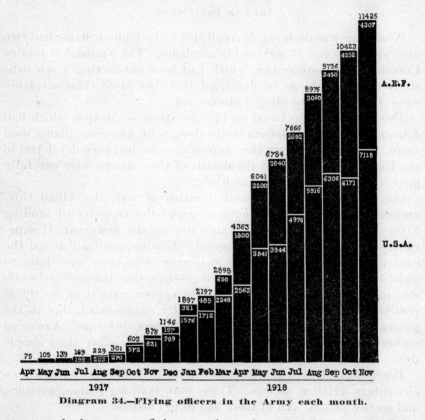

Diagram 34.—Flying officers in the Army each month.

nery, and elementary flying to the point of doing simple flying alone.

Advanced training consisted in the specialized work necessary to qualify the student as a well-prepared all-around pilot or observer, as the case might be, ready to take up and master quickly any type of machine or any kind of observation or bombing duty which the exigencies of the service might necessitate.

Final training, given in Europe, was a short intensive specialization on the particular type of machine, or the particular military problem to which the pilot or observer was finally assigned.

The initial shortage of instructors and the opening of new fields made it necessary to retain a considerable proportion of the early graduating classes as instructors. At the date of the armistice there were 27 fields in operation, with 1,063 instructors; 8,602 men had been graduated from elementary training, and 4,028 from advanced training. There were then actually in training 6,528 men, of whom 59 per cent were in elementary, and 41 per cent in advanced training schools.

There had been sent to the expeditionary forces more than 5,000 pilots and observers of whom, at the date of armistice, 2,226 were still in training, and 1,238 were on flying duty at the front.

Diagram 34 shows the number of flying officers in the Army from month to month.

The columns show the whole number in service each month and the upper portions the numbers of those who were in service overseas. The total personnel of our Air Service, including flying and nonflying officers, students, and enlisted men, increased from about 1,200 at the outbreak of the war to nearly 200,000 at the close.

TRAINING PLANES AND ENGINES.

With 5,000 aviators demanded and only 55 training planes on hand, the production of training planes was the problem of greatest immediate concern. A few planes provided for in the 1917 fiscal appropriation were on order. Other orders were rapidly placed. Deliveries of primary training planes were begun in June, 1917. To the date of the armistice over 5,300 had been produced, including 1,600 of a type which was abandoned on account of unsatisfactory engines.

Advanced training planes reached quantity production early in 1918; up to the armistice about 2,500 were delivered. Approximately the same number were purchased overseas for training the units with the expeditionary force. Diagram 35 shows the production of training planes and engines by months.

European experience had demonstrated that the maintenance of a squadron, whether in training or in service, requires more engines than planes for replacements. Pending the results of American experience, British figures, requiring an average production of two engines per plane, were adopted as standard for American computations. Extensive orders were placed for two types of elementary and three types of advanced training engines.

The upper line in the diagram shows that quantity production of training engines was reached in 1917, and that by the end of November, 1918, a total of nearly 18,000 training engines and more than 9,500 training planes had been delivered. Of the engines, all but 1,346 were built in the United States; and of the 9,500 training planes, more than 8,000 were of American manufacture.

SERVICE PLANES.

As soon as war was declared it became possible for American officers and engineers to learn the secrets of the great improvements that had been developed during the war in the design of airplanes used in battle service. A commission was immediately sent abroad to

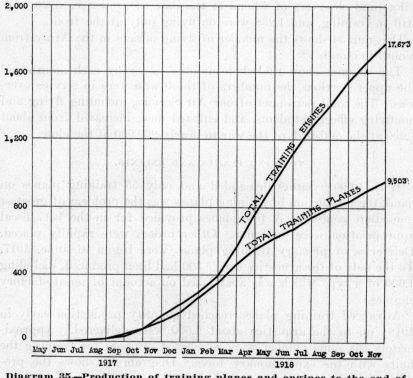

Diagram 35.—**Production of training planes and engines to the end of each month.**

select types of foreign service planes for production in the United States.

A controlling factor in their selections was the necessity of redesigning the models so as to take American-made motors, as foreign engine production was insufficient to meet even the needs of the Allies.

Because of this and because of the rapidity with which the designs of the smaller planes were changing, the best allied authorities urged the concentration of American production on the more stable observation and bombing machines, leaving the production of pursuit planes to the European factories, which were in closer contact with the front. In the case of any plane selected only an estimate could be made as to its probable adaptability to a new type of motor, this engineering risk being less in the more conservative types of design. This consideration, together with the imperative need for quick large-scale production, led to the selection of four types for this experiment: The De Havilland–4 (British) observation and day-bombing

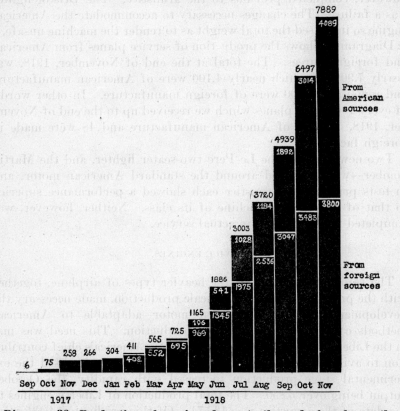

Diagram 36.—Production of service planes to the end of each month.

machine, the Handley-Page (British) night bomber, the Caproni (Italian) night bomber, and the Bristol (British) two-seater fighter. This selection was approved by the French and British authorities.

The redesigned De Havilland–4 proved to be a good, all-round plane of rather poor visibility, with a tank design which increased the danger in case of a crash, but with these defects more than compensated by unusually good maneuver ability, and great speed. The De Havillands were acknowledged to be the fastest observation and bombing planes on the western front. At the time of the armistice this plane was being produced at a rate of over 1,100 per month. A total of 3,227 had been completed, 1,885 had been shipped to France, and 667 to the zone of the advance. The Handley-Page was redesigned to take two high-powered American motors, passed its tests, and on the date of the armistice, parts for 100 had been shipped abroad for assembly.

Delay in the receipt of plans for the Caproni greatly retarded the redesign of this machine. Successful tests of the new model were, however, completed previous to the armistice. The Bristol fighter was a failure. The changes necessary to accommodate the American engine so increased the total weight as to render the machine unsafe.

Diagram 36 shows the production of service planes from American and foreign sources. The total at the end of November, 1918, was nearly 7,900, of which nearly 4,100 were of American manufacture, and remaining 3,800 were of foreign manufacture. In other words, of every 100 battle planes which we received up to the end of November, 1918, 52 were of American manufacture and 48 were made in foreign factories.

Two new models—the Le Pere two-seater fighter, and the Martin bomber—were designed around the standard American motor, and in tests prior to the armistice each showed a performance superior to that of any known machine of its class. Neither, however, was completed in time for use in actual service.

SERVICE ENGINES.

The rapid development of the heavier types of airplane, together with the pressing need for large scale production, made necessary the development of a high-powered motor adaptable to American methods of standardized quantity production. This need was met in the Liberty 12-cylinder motor which was America's chief contribution to aviation. After this standardized motor had passed the experimental stage production increased with rapidity, the October output being over 3,850. The total production of Liberty engines to the date of the armistice was 13,574. Of this production 4,435 were shipped overseas to the expeditionary forces and 1,025 were delivered to the British, French, and Italian air services. It is noteworthy that at the present time the British are requesting the delivery of Liberty motors to them in accordance with arrangements made during the war.

Other types of service engines, including the Hispano-Suiza 300 horsepower, the Bugatti, and the Liberty eight-cylinder, were under development when hostilities ceased. The Hispano-Suiza 180 horsepower had reached quantity production; 469 of this type were produced, of which about one-half were shipped overseas for use in foreign-built pursuit planes.

The columns of diagram 37 indicate the total number of service engines produced for the Army to the end of each month, and show how many of them came from American factories and how many from foreign ones.

Up to the end of November, 1918, the total number of service engines secured was in excess of 22,000. Of this number more than 16,000, or 73 per cent, were from American sources and less than 6,000 from foreign sources.

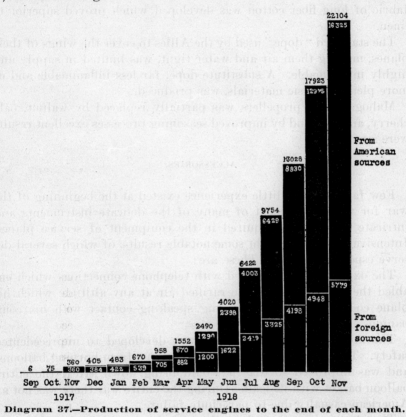

Diagram 37.—Production of service engines to the end of each month.

RAW MATERIALS.

The American and allied airplane programs called for quantities of certain raw materials, which threatened to exhaust the supply. This was true of spruce and fir, lubricating oils, linen, dopes, and mahogany.

In order to meet the spruce and fir shortage labor battalions were organized and placed in the forests of the west coast, loyal organizations of civilian labor were fostered, new kiln processes were developed which seasoned the lumber rapidly, without loss of strength and resiliency. These methods solved the problem. Approximately 174,000,000 feet of spruce and fir were delivered, of which more than two-thirds went to the Allies.

Castor oil was at first the only satisfactory lubricant for airplane motors. The limited supply was far short of the prospective demand, but the situation was met by planting a large acreage of castor beans and the development of a mineral oil substitute.

To meet an acute shortage of linen for the wings of planes a fabric of long fiber cotton was developed which proved superior to linen.

The standard " dope " used by the Allies to cover the wings of their planes, making them air and water tight, was limited in supply and highly inflammable. A substitute dope, far less inflammable and of more plentiful basic materials, was produced.

Mahogany for propellers was partially replaced by walnut, oak, cherry, and ash, and by improved seasoning processes excellent results were secured.

ACCESSORIES.

Few facilities and little experience existed at the beginning of the war for the development of many of the delicate instruments and intricate mechanisms required in the equipment of service planes. Intensive research brought some notable results, of which several deserve especial mention. These are:

The oxygen mask, equipped with telephone connections which enabled the flyer to endure the rarified air at any altitude which his plane could reach without losing speaking contact with his companions.

The military parachute, which was developed to unprecedented safety. This was used principally for escape from burning balloons, and was improved so that it would bring down safely the entire balloon basket with its load. During the entire war there was not an American casualty due to parachute failure.

The electric-heated clothing for aviators on high altitude work. The electric suit, developed in the latter months of the war and used at the front, was lined with insulated coils through which current was driven by means of a small dynamo actuated by a miniature propeller driven by the rush of the plane through the air.

Long-focus, light-filtration cameras by which good photographs could be taken through haze from altitudes of 3 miles or more. Primary credit for this belongs to Europe, but America improved the mechanism and standardized the design for quantity production.

The wireless telephone, by which the aviator is enabled to converse easily with other planes and with ground stations. This development came too late to be of any substantial use at the front, but its value for peace as well as for any future war is obvious.

BALLOONS.

Diagram 38 shows the total number of observation balloons manufactured and the number that were shipped overseas.

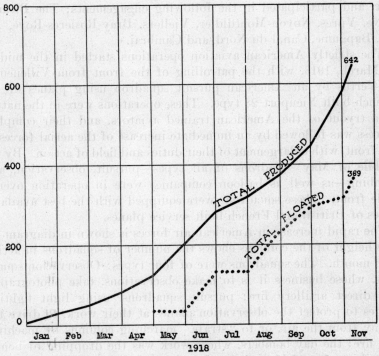

Diagram 38.—Observation balloons produced and shipped overseas each month.

In no field did American manufacturing capacity achieve a greater relative success. Before the armistice we had produced 642 observation balloons and had received 20 from the French. Forty-three of our balloons had been destroyed and 35 given to the French and British.

This left us with 574 balloons at the end of the war. On the same date the Belgian Army had 6, the British 43, the French 72, and the Germans 170 on the western front. These figures mean that at the end of the war we had nearly twice as many observation balloons as the enemy and the Allies combined had at the front.

The American pilots of the Lafayette Escadrille were transferred from the French to the American service December 26, 1917, flying as civilians until formally commissioned in late January, 1918. They were then attached to and served with the French Fourth Army, operating over Rheims.

In addition to the purely American operations, two full squadrons were attached to the British Royal Air Force in March and June respectively, of 1918, remaining with the British throughout the war, and participated in the following engagements: The Picardy drive, Ypres, Noyon-Montdidier, Viellers, Bray-Rosieres-Roye, Arras, Bapaume, Canal du Nord, and Cambrai.

The strictly American aviation operations started in the middle of March, 1918, with the patrolling of the front from Villeneuve-les-Vertus by an American pursuit squadron using planes of the French-built Nieuport-28 type. These operations were in the nature of a tryout of the American trained aviators, and their complete success was followed by an immediate increase of the aerial forces at the front, with enlargement of their duties and field of action. By the middle of May squadrons of all types—pursuit, observation, and bombing—as well as balloon companies were in operation over a wide front. These squadrons were equipped with the best available types of British and French-built service planes.

The rapid increase in American air forces is shown in diagram 39. The height of the columns shows the number of squadrons in action each month. The squadrons were of four types: Observation squadrons, whose business it is to make observations, take photographs, and direct artillery fire; pursuit squadrons, using light fighting planes to protect the observation planes at their work, to drive the enemy from the air, or to "strafe" marching columns by machine-gun fire; the day bombers, whose work was the dropping of bombs on railways or roads; and the night bombers, carrying heavier bomb loads for the destruction of strategic enemy works.

In April the American forces just going into active sectors had three squadrons, two for observation and one for pursuit. Their strength totaled 35 planes. In May, as the diagram shows, the squadrons were increased to nine. The most rapid growth occurred after July, when American De Havilland planes were becoming available in quantity for observation and day bombing service, and by November the number of squadrons increased to 45, with a total of 740 planes in action.

The equipment of American squadrons was in the early months entirely of French and British manufacture. American De Havilland–4 planes were first used at the front on August 7, and the number in service increased rapidly from that time on.

The total number of service planes that had been sent to the zone of advance by the end of each month for the use of American airmen with our armies is shown in diagram 40. The upper portion of the columns represents planes of American make, and the lower portion planes of foreign make. Of the total 2,698 planes sent to the zone of advance, 667, or one-quarter, were of American make and the proportion was rapidly increasing at the time of the signing of the armistice.

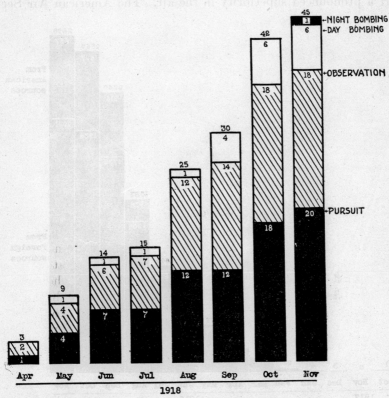

Diagram 39.—American air squadrons in action each month.

Of the 2,031 planes from foreign sources sent forward about nine-tenths were French. The planes sent to the zone of advance are approximately one-half of the service planes received by the A. E. F., the other half being in back areas.

The rapid rate of destruction of planes at the front is illustrated by the fact that out of the 2,698 planes dispatched to the zone of advance about 1,100 remained at the time of the signing of the armistice.

IMPORTANT OPERATIONS.

Three major operations, marking the critical points in American participation in the war, also furnish a comparison indicating the growth of American air forces in action. These are: The Second Battle of the Marne, St. Mihiel, and the Meuse-Argonne.

CHATEAU-THIERRY—JULY.

On the Chateau-Thierry-Soissons front the Germans had at the start a pronounced superiority in the air. The American Air Serv-

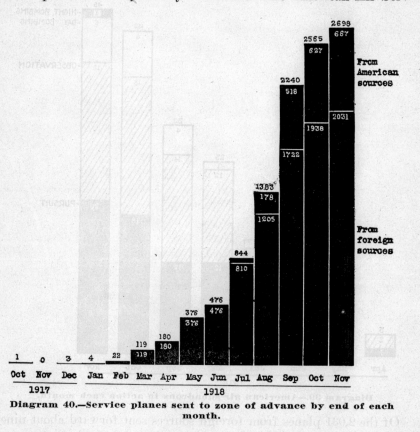

Diagram 40.—Service planes sent to zone of advance by end of each month.

ice succeeded, however, in establishing the lines of contact with enemy airmen from 3 to 10 miles within the enemy's lines, photographed the entire front and the terrain deep behind the lines, and played an important part in putting German air forces on the defensive. The German concentration for the attack of July 15 was reported in detail and the location of the German reserves established, while the secrecy of the allied mobilization for the counterattack was maintained and the Germans surprised. The American force employed consisted of four pursuit squadrons, three observation squadrons and three balloon companies.

ST. MIHIEL—SEPTEMBER.

In capturing the St. Mihiel salient the American first army was aided and protected by the largest concentration of air force ever made, of which approximately one-third were American and the other two-thirds were French, British, and Italian squadrons operating under American command. Throughout this operation the German back areas were kept under bombardment day and night; their reserves and ammunition dumps were located for the American long-range artillery; propaganda designed to disaffect enemy personnel was dropped; record was made by photograph of every movement of the enemy's lines and reserves, such information being frequently delivered to headquarters in finished photographs within half an hour of its occurrence; and fast pursuit planes armed with machine guns flew low over the German lines, firing directly into his infantry.

Day bombers and corps and artillery observers were forced to fly low on account of the fog which hampered all the day operations, greatly reduced the visibility, and made infantry liaison especially difficult. This accounts for the fact that some trouble was experienced by the Infantry with German "strafing" planes.

The American air force employed consisted of 12 pursuit squadrons, 11 observation squadrons, 3 bombing squadrons, and 14 balloon companies. This large force performed an amount of flying approximately three times as great as was done during the Chateau-Thierry operations. Diagram 41 shows the number of hours spent in the air each week by American service planes at the front. During the last two weeks of July the flying time was more than 1,000 hours per week. The week of the St. Mihiel offensive it rose to nearly 4,000 hours.

MEUSE-ARGONNE—SEPTEMBER TO NOVEMBER.

Because the Meuse-Argonne engagement covered a wider front and a more extended period of time, against an enemy who had improved his distribution of air force along the entire southern section of the front, no such heavy instantaneous concentration of planes as was made at St. Mihiel was possible. In this operation, moreover, less assistance was rendered by French and British flyers. The American force used during the engagement was considerably larger than at St. Mihiel.

During the six weeks' struggle, the losses were heavy, but replacements were brought forward so rapidly that at the last stage
of the action the available American strength was greater than at the
start. As shown by diagram 41, American air activities continued
during the Argonne fighting on the same scale as during the St.
Mihiel offensive.

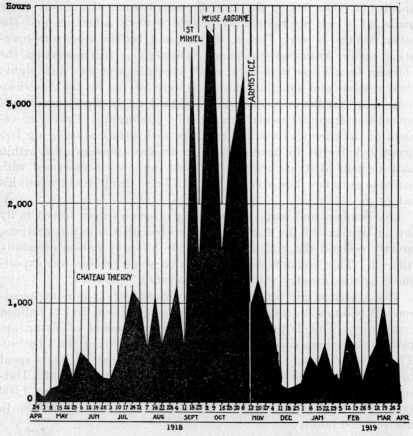

**Diagram 41.—Hours spent in the air each week by American service
planes at the front.**

STRENGTH AT ARMISTICE.

At the signing of the armistice, there were on the front 20 pursuit
squadrons, 18 observation squadrons, and 7 squadrons of bombers;
with 1,238 flying officers and 740 service planes. There were also 23
balloon companies.

THE TEST OF BATTLE.

The final test of the American Air Service is the test of battle.
The final record is the record of the results of combat. Casualty

figures are an important part of the record. American aviators brought down in the course of their few months of active service 755 enemy planes. Our losses in combat were 357 planes. This is illustrated in diagram 42. The record of our balloon companies shows a somewhat less favorable comparison between our own and enemy

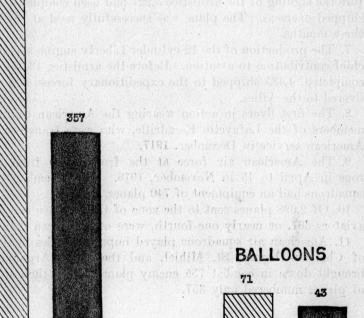

AIRPLANES

755

357

BALLOONS

71

43

| Enemy by American | American by enemy | | Enemy by American | American by enemy |

Diagram 42.—Airplanes and balloons brought down in action.

losses, the figures being 43 American and 71 German balloons destroyed.

SUMMARY.

1. On the declaration of war the United States had 55 training airplanes, of which 51 were classified as obsolete and the other 4 as obsolescent.

2. When we entered the war the Allies made the designs of their planes available to us and before the end of hostilities furnished us from their own manufacture 3,800 service planes.

3. Aviation training schools in the United States graduated 8,602 men from elementary courses and 4,028 from advanced courses. More than 5,000 pilots and observers were sent overseas.

4. The total personnel of the Air Service, officers, students, and enlisted men, increased from 1,200 at the outbreak of the war to nearly 200,000 at its close.

5. There were produced in the United States to November 30, 1918, more than 8,000 training planes and more than 16,000 training engines.

6. The De Havilland–4 observation and day bombing plane was the only plane the United States put into quantity production. Before the signing of the armistice 3,227 had been completed and 1,885 shipped overseas. The plane was successfully used at the front for three months.

7. The production of the 12-cylinder Liberty engine was America's chief contribution to aviation. Before the armistice 13,574 had been completed, 4,435 shipped to the expeditionary forces, and 1,025 delivered to the Allies.

8. The first flyers in action wearing the American uniform were members of the Lafayette Escadrille, who were transferred to the American service in December, 1917.

9. The American air force at the front grew from 3 squadrons in April to 45 in November, 1918. On November 11 the 45 squadrons had an equipment of 740 planes.

10. Of 2,698 planes sent to the zone of the advance for American aviators 667, or nearly one-fourth, were of American manufacture.

11. American air squadrons played important rôles in the battles of Chateau-Thierry, St. Mihiel, and the Meuse-Argonne. They brought down in combat 755 enemy planes, while their own losses of planes numbered only 357.

Chapter VIII.

TWO HUNDRED DAYS OF BATTLE.

TWO OUT OF THREE.

Two out of every three American soldiers who reached France took part in battle. The number who reached France was 2,084,000, and of these 1,390,000 saw active service in the front line.

American combat forces were organized into divisions, which, as has been noted, consisted of some 28,000 officers and men. These divisions were the largest on the western front, since the British division numbered about 15,000 and those of the French and Germans about 12,000 each. There were sent overseas 42 American divisions and several hundred thousand supplementary artillery and service of supply troops. Diagram 43 shows the numerical designations of the American divisions that were in France each month. The numbers in the columns are the numbers of the divisions in France each month, and in every case the numbers of those arriving during the month are placed at the top of the column, while those designating the divisions already there are shown below.

Of the 42 divisions that reached France 29 took part in active combat service, while the others were used for replacements or were just arriving during the last month of hostilities. The battle record of the United States Army in this war is largely the history of these 29 combat divisions. Seven of them were Regular Army divisions, 11 were organized from the National Guard, and 11 were made up of National Army troops.

American combat divisions were in battle for 200 days, from the 25th of April, 1918, when the first Regular division after long training in quiet sectors, entered an active sector on the Picardy front, until the signing of the armistice. During these 200 days they were engaged in 13 major operations, of which 11 were joint enterprises with the French, British, and Italians, and 2 were distinctively American.

At the time of their greatest activity in the second week of October all 29 American divisions were in action. They then held 101 miles of front, or 23 per cent of the entire allied battle line. From the middle of August until the end of the war they held, during the greater part of the time, a front longer than that held by the British. Their strength tipped the balance of man power in favor of the Allies, so that from the middle of June, 1918, to the end of the war the allied forces were superior in number to those of the enemy.

```
                                                                   8
                                                                  38
                                                                  31
                                                              34  34
                                                              86  86
                                                              84  84
                                                              87  87
                                                          40  40  40
                                                          39  39  39
                                                          88  88  88
                                                          81  81  81
                                                           7   7   7
                                                          85  85  85
                                                      36  36  36  36
                                                      91  91  91  91
                                                      79  79  79  79
                                                      76  76  76  76
                                                  29  29  29  29  29
                                                  37  37  37  37  37
                                                  90  90  90  90  90
                                                  92  92  92  92  92
                                                  89  89  89  89  89
                                                  83  83  83  83  83
                                                  78  78  78  78  78
                                              80  80  80  80  80  80
                                              30  30  30  30  30  30
                                              33  33  33  33  33  33
                                               6   6   6   6   6   6
                                              27  27  27  27  27  27
                                               4   4   4   4   4   4
                                              28  28  28  28  28  28
                                              35  35  35  35  35  35
                                              82  82  82  82  82  82
                                          77  77  77  77  77  77  77
                                           3   3   3   3   3   3   3
                                           5   5   5   5   5   5   5
                                  32  32  32  32  32  32  32  32  32
                              41  41  41  41  41  41  41  41  41  41
                          42  42  42  42  42  42  42  42  42  42  42
              26  26  26  26  26  26  26  26  26  26  26  26  26  26
               2   2   2   2   2   2   2   2   2   2   2   2   2   2
           1   1   1   1   1   1   1   1   1   1   1   1   1   1   1
        Jun Jul Aug Sep Oct Nov Dec  Jan Feb Mar Apr May Jun Jul Aug Sep Oct
                      1917                        1918
```

Diagram 43.—Numerical designations of American divisions in France each month.

The total battle advances of all the American divisions amount to 782 kilometers, or 485 miles, an average advance for each division of 17 miles, nearly all of it against desperate enemy resistance. They captured 63,000 prisoners, 1,378 pieces of artillery, 708 trench mortars, and 9,650 machine guns. In June and July they helped to shatter the enemy advance toward Paris and to turn retreat into a triumphant offensive. At St. Mihiel they pinched off in a day an

enemy salient which had been a constant menace to the French line
for four years.   In the Argonne and on the Meuse they carried lines
which the enemy was determined to hold at any cost, and cut the
enemy lines of communication and supply for half the western
battle front.

The maps and diagrams in this chapter show in more detail the
part American troops played in the allied endeavor, something of

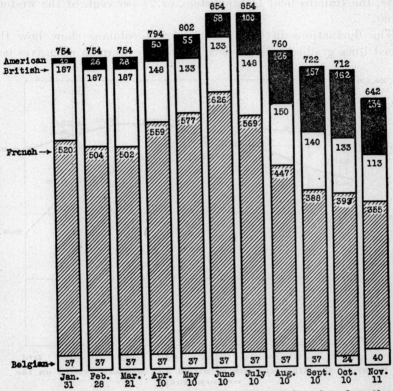

Diagram 44.—Kilometers of front line held by armies of each nation.

the scale and character of their operations, and several comparative
records of the 29 combat divisions.

TIPPING THE BALANCE OF POWER.

The place American troops took in the allied undertaking is
illustrated in diagram 44, which shows in kilometers the length of
front line held by the armies of each nation on the allied side
during the year 1918. In January American troops were holding
10 kilometers, or 6¼ miles, of front in quiet sectors. In April their
line had lengthened to 50 kilometers. In July this figure was

doubled and in September tripled. The high point was reached
in October, with 29 divisions in line, extending over a front of 162
kilometers, or 101 miles, nearly one-quarter of the entire western
front. These changes are shown on the diagram in the upper
portions of the columns in solid black.

The length of front shown as occupied by the French includes
the lines held by the Italian Second Army Corps. On November 11,
1918, the Italians held 14 kilometers, or 2⅓ per cent, of the western
front.

The fluctuations in the heights of the columns show how the
allied lines gradually lengthened as the five German offensives bel-

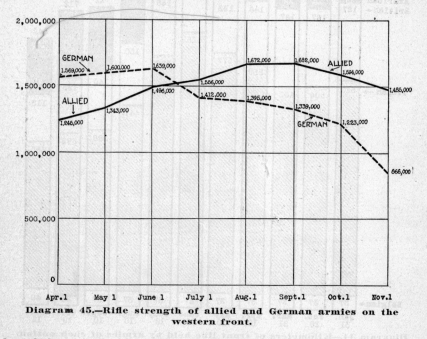

**Diagram 45.—Rifle strength of allied and German armies on the
western front.**

lowed them out in big salients and rapidly shortened as the German
retreats began.

Another measure of American participation is the effect caused by
the rapid arrivals of American troops on the rifle strength of the
allied armies. One of the best indexes of effective man power is
the number of riflemen ready for front-line service. For example,
there are 12,250 rifles in an American division and smaller numbers in those of other armies.

Diagram 45 shows the rifle strength of the allied and German
armies on the western front from April 1 to November 1, 1918.

The dotted line shows the German rifle strength at the beginning
of each month and the solid line the allied strength. On the 1st of

April the Germans had an actual superiority of 324,000 riflemen on the western front. Their strength increased during the next two months but began to drop during June. At the same time the allied strength, with the constantly growing American forces, was showing a steady increase, so that the two lines crossed during June. From that time on allied strength was always in the ascendency and since the French and British forces were weaker in October and November than they were in April and May, this growing ascendency of the Allies was due entirely to the Americans. By November 1 the allied rifle strength had a superiority over the German of more than 600,000 rifles.

THIRTEEN BATTLES.

American troops saw service on practically every stretch of the western front from British lines in Belgium to inactive sectors in the Vosges. On October 21, 1917, Americans entered the line in the quiet Toul sector. From that date to the armistice American units were somewhere in line almost continuously.

It is difficult to cut up the year and 22 days which intervened into well-defined battles, for in a sense the entire war on the western front was a single battle. It is possible, however, to distinguish certain major operations or phases of the greater struggle. Thirteen such operations have been recognized in which American units were engaged, of which 12 took place on the western front and 1 in Italy. Battle clasps will be awarded to the officers and men who participated in these engagements. These battles are named and the number of Americans engaged is shown in table 7, on this page.

TABLE 7.—*Thirteen major operations in which Americans participated.*

Operation.	Approximate number of Americans engaged.
West front—Campaign of 1917:	
Cambrai, Nov. 20 to Dec. 4	2,500
West front—Campaign of 1918:	
German offensives, Mar. 21 to July 18—	
Somme, Mar. 21 to Apr. 6	2,200
Lys, Apr. 9 to 27	500
Aisne, May 27 to June 5	27,500
Noyon-Montdidier, June 9 to 15	27,000
Champagne-Marne, July 15 to 18	85,000
Allied offensives, July 18 to Nov. 11—	
Aisne-Marne, July 18 to Aug. 6	270,000
Somme, Aug. 8 to Nov. 11	54,000
Oise-Aisne, Aug. 18 to Nov. 11	85,000
Ypres-Lys, Aug. 19 to Nov. 11	108,000
St. Mihiel, Sept. 12 to 16	550,000
Meuse-Argonne, Sept. 20 to Nov. 11	1,200,000
Italian front—Campaign of 1918:	
Vittorio-Veneto, Oct. 24 to Nov. 4	1,200

The first major operation in which American troops were engaged was the Cambrai battle at the end of the campaign of 1917. Scattering medical and engineering detachments, serving with the British, were present during the action but sustained no serious casualties.

GERMAN OFFENSIVES.

The campaign of 1918 opened with the Germans in possession of the offensive. In a series of five drives of unprecedented violence the

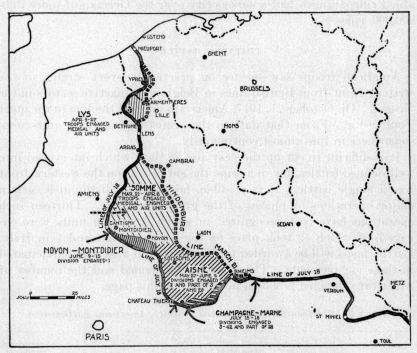

Map 9.—The five great German offensives of 1918.

imperial Great General Staff sought to break the allied line and end the war. These five drives took place in five successive months, beginning in March. Each drive was so timed as to take advantage of the light of the moon for that month. Map 9, on this page, shows the ground won by the Germans in each of the offensives. The arrows indicate the points at which American troops went into the battle, and the small numbers are the numerical designations of the American divisions taking part.

The first drive opened on March 21, on a 50-mile front across the old battle field of the Somme. In 17 days of fighting the Germans advanced their lines beyond Noyon and Montdidier and were within

12 miles of the important railroad center of Amiens with its great stores of British supplies. In this battle, also known as the Picardy offensive, approximately 2,200 American troops, serving with the British and French, were engaged.

The attack upon Amiens had been but partially checked when the enemy struck again to the north in the Armentieres sector and advanced for 17 miles up the valley of the Lys. A small number of Americans, serving with the British, participated in the Lys defensive.

For their next attack (May 27) the Germans selected the French front along the Chemin des Dames north of the Aisne. The line from Rheims to a little east of Noyon was forced back. Soissons fell, and on May 31 the enemy had reached the Marne Valley, down which he was advancing in the direction of Paris. At this critical moment our Second Division, together with elements of the Third and Twenty-eighth Divisions were thrown into the line. By blocking the German advance at Chateau-Thierry, they rendered great assistance in stopping perhaps the most dangerous of the German drives. The Second Division not only halted the enemy on its front but also recaptured from him the strong tactical positions of Bouresches, Belleau Wood, and Vaux.

The enemy had by his offensives established two salients threatening Paris. He now sought to convert them into one by a fourth terrific blow delivered on a front of 22 miles between Montdidier and Noyon. The reinforced French Army resisted firmly and the attack was halted after an initial advance of about 6 miles. Throughout this operation (June 9–15) the extreme left line of the salient was defended by our First Division. Even before the drive began the division had demonstrated the fighting qualities of our troops by capturing and holding the town of Cantigny (May 28).

There followed a month of comparative quiet, during which the enemy reassembled his forces for his fifth onslaught. On July 15 he attacked simultaneously on both sides of Rheims, the eastern corner of the salient he had created in the Aisne drive. To the east of the city he gained little. On the west he crossed the Marne, but made slight progress. His path was everywhere blocked. In this battle 85,000 American troops were engaged—the Forty-second division to the extreme east in Champagne, and the Third and Twenty-eighth to the west, near Chateau-Thierry.

ALLIED OFFENSIVES.

The turning point of the war had come. The great German offensives had been stopped. The initiative now passed from Ludendorff to Marshal Foch, and a series of allied offensives began, des-

tined to roll back the German armies beyond the French frontier.
In this continuous allied offensive there may be distinguished six
phases or major operations in which the American Expeditionary
Forces took part.

These six operations are shown on map 10, on this page, in which
the solid arrows indicate points where American divisions entered
the line, and the broken arrows the distances over which they drove
forward. In four of the six operations the American troops engaged were acting in support of allied divisions and under the command of the generals of the Allies.

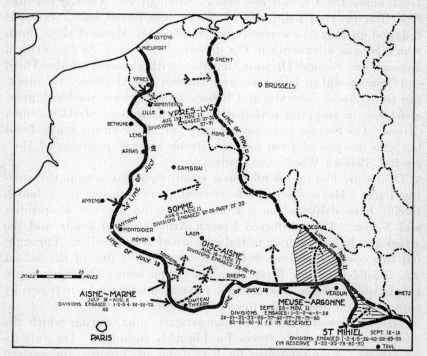

Map 10.—American participation in the allied offensives of 1918.

The moment chosen by Marshal Foch for launching the first
counteroffensive was July 18, when it was clear that the German
Champagne-Marne drive had spent its force. The place chosen was
the uncovered west flank of the German salient from the Aisne to
the Marne. The First, Second, Third, Fourth, Twenty-sixth, Twenty-
eighth, Thirty-second, and Forty-second American Divisions, together with selected French troops, were employed. When the operation was completed (August 6) the salient had been flattened out
and the allied line ran from Soissons to Rheims along the Vesle.

Two days later the British struck at the Somme salient, initiating
an offensive which, with occasional breathing spells, lasted to the

date of the armistice. American participation in this operation was intermittent. From August 8 to 20 elements of the Thirty-third Division, which had been brigaded for training with the Australians, were in the line and took part in the capture of Chipilly Ridge. Later the Twenty-seventh and Thirtieth Divisions, who served throughout with the British, were brought over from the Ypres sector and used in company with Australian troops to break the Hindenburg line at the tunnel of the St. Quentin Canal (Sept. 20–Oct. 20).

In the meantime simultaneous assaults were in progress at other points on the front. On August 18 Gen. Mangin began the Oise-Aisne phase of the great allied offensive. Starting from the Soissons-Rheims line, along which they had come to rest August 6, the French armies advanced by successive stages to the Aisne, to Laon, and on November 11 were close to the frontier. In the first stages of this advance they were assisted by the Twenty-eighth, Thirty-second, and Seventh-seventh American Divisions, but by September 15 all of these were withdrawn for the coming Meuse-Argonne offensive of the American Army.

The day after the opening of the Oise-Aisne offensive the British launched the first of a series of attacks in the Ypres sector which continued with some interruptions to the time of the armistice and may be termed the "Ypres-Lys offensive." Four American divisions at different times participated in this operation. The Twenty-seventh and Thirtieth were engaged in the recapture of Mount Kemmel August 31 to September 2. The Thirty-seventh and Ninety-first were withdrawn from the Meuse-Argonne battle and dispatched to Belgium, where they took part in the last stages of the Ypres-Lys offensive (Oct. 31 to Nov. 11).

With the organization of the American First Army on August 10, under the personal command of Gen. Pershing, the history of the American Expeditionary Forces entered upon a new stage. The St. Mihiel (Sept. 12–16) and Meuse-Argonne (Sept. 26–Nov. 11) offensives were major operation planned and executed by American generals and American troops. The ground won in each is shown by the shaded areas in map 10.

In addition to the 12 operations above mentioned, American troops participated in the Battle of Vittorio-Veneto (Oct. 24 to Nov. 4), which ended in the rout of the Austrian Army.

THE BATTLE OF ST. MIHIEL.

The first distinctly American offensive was the reduction of the St. Mihiel salient carried through from September 12 to September 15, largely by American troops and wholly under the orders of the American commander in chief. The positions of the various American divisions at the beginning of the offensive and on each succeeding day are shown on map 11 on this page. The arrows indicate the advance of each division. In the attack the American troops were aided by French colonial troops, who held the portion of the front line shown in dashes on the left of the map. The Americans were also aided by French and British air squadrons.

The attack began at 5 a. m., after four hours of artillery preparation of great severity, and met with immediate success. Before noon about half the distance between the bases of the salient had been

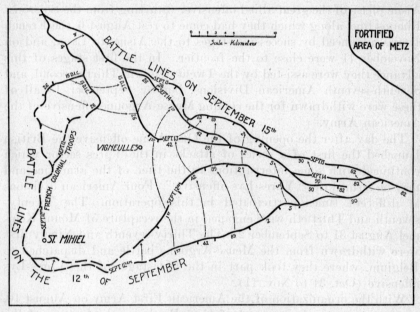

Map 11.—The Battle of St. Mihiel.

covered and the next morning troops of the First and Twenty-sixth Divisions met at Vigneulles, cutting off the salient within 24 hours from the beginning of the movement.

Two comparisons between this operation and the Battle of Gettysburg emphasize the magnitude of the action. About 550,000 Americans were engaged at St. Mihiel; the Union forces at Gettysburg numbered approximately 100,000. St. Mihiel set a record for concentration of artillery fire by a four-hour artillery preparation, consuming more than 1,000,000 rounds of ammunition. In three days at Gettysburg Union artillery fired 33,000 rounds.

The St. Mihiel offensive cost only about 7,000 casualties, less than one-third the Union losses at Gettysburg. There were captured 16,000 prisoners and 443 guns. A dangerous enemy salient was reduced, and American commanders and troops demonstrated their ability to plan and execute a big American operation.

THE BATTLE OF THE MEUSE-ARGONNE.

The object of the Meuse-Argonne offensive, said Gen. Pershing in his report of November 20, 1918, was " to draw the best German divisions to our front and to consume them." This sentence expresses better than any long description not only the object but also the outcome of the battle. Every available American division was thrown against the enemy. Every available German division was thrown in to meet them. At the end of 47 days of continuous battle our divisions had consumed the German divisions.

The goal of the American attack was the Sedan-Meziéres railroad, the main line of supply for the German forces on the major part of the western front. If this line were cut, a retirement on the whole front would be forced. This retirement would include, moreover, evacuation of the Briey iron fields, which the Germans had been using to great advantage to supplement their iron supply. The defense of the positions threatened was therefore of such importance as to warrant the most desperate measures for resistance. When the engagement was evidently impending the commander of the German Fifth Army sent word to his forces, calling on them for unyielding resistance and pointing out that defeat in this engagement might mean disaster for the fatherland.

Map 12 shows the progress of the American action, giving the lines held by divisions on different days. On the first day, the 26th of September, and the next day or two after that, the lines were considerably advanced. Then the resistance became more stubborn. Each side threw in more and more of its man power until there were no more reserves. Many German divisions went into action twice, and not a few three times, until, through losses, they were far under strength. All through the month of October the attrition went on. Foot by foot American troops pushed back the best of the German divisions. On November 1 the last stage of the offensive began. The enemy power began to break. American troops forced their way to the east bank of the Meuse. Toward the north they made even more rapid progress, and in seven days reached the outskirts of Sedan and cut the Sedan-Meziéres railroad, making the German line untenable.

In the meantime (Oct. 2 to 28) our Second and Thirty-sixth Divisions had been sent west to assist the French who were advancing in Champagne beside our drive in the Argonne. The liaison detachment between the two armies was for a time furnished by the Ninety-second Division.

In some ways the Meuse-Argonne offers an interesting resemblance
to the Battle of the Wilderness, fought from May 5 to 12, 1864, in
the Civil War. Both were fought over a terrain covered with tangled
woods and underbrush. The Wilderness was regarded as a long battle, marked by slow progress, against obstinate resistance, with very
heavy casualties. Here the similarity ends. The Meuse-Argonne

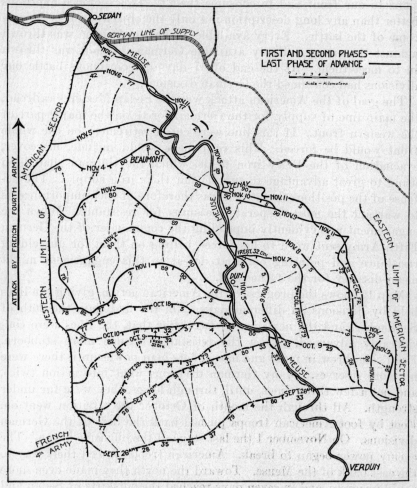

Map 12.—The Battle of the Meuse-Argonne.

lasted six times as long as the Battle of the Wilderness. Twelve
times as many American troops were engaged as were on the Union
side. They used in the action ten times as many guns and fired
about one hundred times as many rounds of artillery ammunition.
The actual weight of the ammunition fired was greater than that used
by the Union forces during the entire Civil War. Casualties were

perhaps four times as heavy as among the Northern troops in the Battle of the Wilderness.

The Battle of the Meuse-Argonne was beyond compare the greatest ever fought by American troops, and there have been few, if any, greater battles in the history of the world. Some of the more important statistics of the engagement are presented in Table 8.

TABLE 8.—*American data for the Meuse-Argonne Battle.*

Days of battle	47
American troops engaged	1, 200, 000
Guns employed in attack	2, 417
Rounds of artillery ammunition fired	4, 214, 000
Airplanes used	840
Tons of explosives dropped by planes on enemy lines	100
Tanks used	324
Miles of penetration of enemy line, maximum	34
Square kilometers of territory taken	1, 550
Villages and towns liberated	150
Prisoners captured	16, 059
Artillery pieces captured	468
Machine guns captured	2, 864
Trench mortars captured	177
American casualties	120, 000

RECORD OF 29 COMBAT DIVISIONS.

Twenty-nine combat divisions achieved the successes and bore the losses of active operations. The story of their achievements can not be told within the limits of this account. There are, however, certain fundamental records which give us a picture of the accomplishments of these divisions. They tell us how long each division served in the front line; how far each advanced against the enemy; how many prisoners each captured; and how heavily each suffered.

The length of service of each division in quiet and in active sectors of the line is shown in diagram 46. The First Division was the first in line and the first to enter an active sector. It reached France in June, 1917, went into line in October and into an active sector in April, 1918. The next three divisions in order of length of service all reached France in 1917.

Three of the 29 divisions were still serving their apprenticeship and had not seen much severe battle service at the time of the signing of the armistice. They were the Sixth, the Eighty-first, and the Eighty-eighth. It is interesting that of the total of 2,234 days which American divisions spent in line, four-tenths were in active sectors.

Diagram 47 pictures the accomplishments of different divisions by showing the number of kilometers each advanced against the enemy,

and in graphic form the percentage of the total kilometers advanced
which was carried through by each division. The length of the advance depends in each case on the length of service of the division,
the duty assigned to it (whether offensive or defensive), the nature
of the terrain to be covered, the strength and effectiveness of oppos-
ing enemy forces, artillery support, etc. Hence, conclusions as to the
relative efficiency of divisions can not be drawn from these figures
alone.

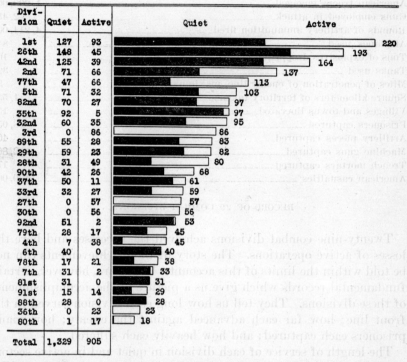

Divi-sion	Quiet	Active	Quiet	Active
1st	127	93		220
26th	148	45		193
42nd	125	39		164
2nd	71	66		137
77th	47	66		113
5th	71	32		103
82nd	70	27		97
35th	92	5		97
32nd	60	35		95
3rd	0	86		86
89th	55	28		83
29th	59	23		82
28th	31	49		80
90th	42	26		68
37th	50	11		61
33rd	32	27		59
27th	0	57		57
30th	0	56		56
92nd	51	2		53
79th	28	17		45
4th	7	38		45
6th	40	0		40
78th	17	21		38
7th	31	2		33
81st	31	0		31
91st	15	14		29
88th	28	0		28
36th	0	23		23
80th	1	17		18
Total	1,329	905		

Diagram 46.—Days spent by each division in quiet and active sectors.

The Seventy-seventh National Army Division, composed largely
of troops from New York City, made the greatest advance—a total
of 71½ kilometers, or nearly 45 miles. This was more than 9 per
cent of the ground gained by the divisions. If the advances are
turned into miles the total advance is 485 miles, and the average gain
for each division 17 miles.

Diagram 48 on the number of German prisoners captured is sub-
ject to the same qualifications as the preceding diagram. The figures
for number of prisoners taken are from the official records of the
different divisions. The total is somewhat higher than the rolls of
American prisoner stockades have shown, but the difference is prob-

ably in prisoners turned over to the French or British. The total number of Americans taken prisoner by Germans was 4,480.

The price paid for these achievements was 256,000 battle casualties; a heavy price when counted in terms of the individuals who gave their lives or suffered from wounds; a small price when compared with the enormous price paid by the nations at whose sides we fought. Diagram 49 gives the roll of honor of the divisions for battle casualties.

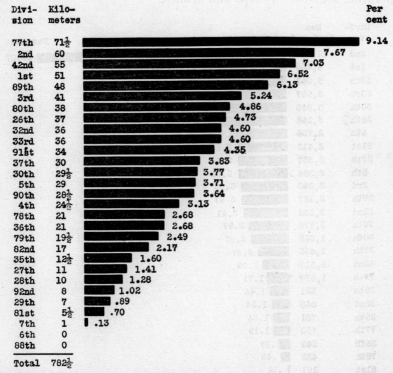

Divi-sion	Kilo-meters	Per cent
77th	71½	9.14
2nd	60	7.67
42nd	55	7.03
1st	51	6.52
89th	48	6.13
3rd	41	5.24
80th	38	4.86
26th	37	4.73
32nd	36	4.60
33rd	36	4.60
91st	34	4.35
37th	30	3.83
30th	29½	3.77
5th	29	3.71
90th	28½	3.64
4th	24½	3.13
78th	21	2.68
36th	21	2.68
79th	19½	2.49
82nd	17	2.17
35th	12½	1.60
27th	11	1.41
28th	10	1.28
92nd	8	1.02
29th	7	.89
81st	5½	.70
7th	1	.13
6th	0	
88th	0	
Total	782½	

Diagram 47.—Kilometers advanced against the enemy by each division.

The figures given were corrected to June 3 and constitute the final record of the office of the adjutant general of the expeditionary forces. Battle deaths include both killed in action and died of wounds. Under wounded are included many slightly injured. Artillery brigade losses are included in the figures of the divisions to which they were originally assigned.

Under "others" are grouped the casualties of several different kinds of units. These are the following.

Others.	Killed.	Wounded.	Total.
Troops not in divisions...	1,019	3,496	4,515
Ninety-third Division..	584	2,582	3,166
Replacement and depot divisions..	690	1,556	2,246
Divisional deaths not distributed......................................	782	....	782
Total...	3,075	7,634	10,709

The troops not in divisions were largely artillery, headquarters, train, and other special services attached to groups of divisions operating together in corps and armies.

Division	Men Captured		Per cent
2nd	12,026		19.07
1st	6,469		10.26
89th	5,061		8.02
33rd	3,987		6.32
30th	3,848		6.10
26th	3,148		4.99
4th	2,756		4.37
91st	2,412		3.82
27th	2,357		3.74
5th	2,356		3.74
3rd	2,240		3.55
29th	2,187		3.47
32nd	2,153		3.41
90th	1,876		2.97
80th	1,813		2.87
37th	1,495		2.37
42nd	1,317		2.09
79th	1,077		1.71
28th	921		1.46
82nd	845		1.34
35th	781		1.24
77th	750		1.19
36th	549		.87
78th	432		.68
81st	101		.16
7th	69		.11
92nd	38		.06
6th	12		.02
88th	3		.00
Total	63,079		

Diagram 48.—German prisoners captured by each division.

The Ninety-third Division is worthy of special comment. It has not been listed among the combat divisions because it was always incomplete as a division. It was without its artillery and some other units, and was brigaded with the French from the time of its arrival in France in the spring of 1918 until the signing of the armistice. Its service in the line was fully as long as that of many of the so-called combat divisions. This is indicated by a comparison of its casualties with those in the other divisions. The division was made up of colored soldiers from National Guard units of various States.

Casualties in replacement and depot divisions are partly accounted for in two ways. In the first place the artillery of a number of these divisions went into action separately. Secondly, some replacement units joining combat divisions suffered casualties before

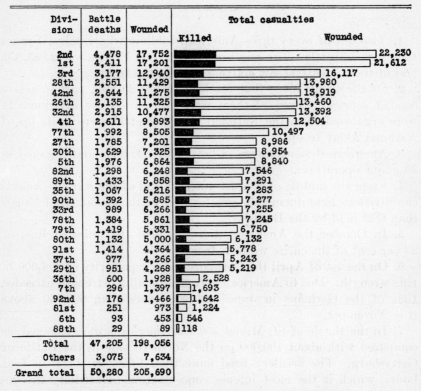

Division	Battle deaths	Wounded	Total casualties Killed	Wounded
2nd	4,478	17,752		22,230
1st	4,411	17,201		21,612
3rd	3,177	12,940		16,117
28th	2,551	11,429		13,980
42nd	2,644	11,275		13,919
26th	2,135	11,325		13,460
32nd	2,915	10,477		13,392
4th	2,611	9,893		12,504
77th	1,992	8,505		10,497
27th	1,785	7,201		8,986
30th	1,629	7,325		8,954
5th	1,976	6,864		8,840
82nd	1,298	6,248		7,546
89th	1,433	5,858		7,291
35th	1,067	6,216		7,283
90th	1,392	5,885		7,277
33rd	989	6,266		7,255
78th	1,384	5,861		7,245
79th	1,419	5,331		6,750
80th	1,132	5,000		6,132
91st	1,414	4,364		5,778
37th	977	4,266		5,243
29th	951	4,268		5,219
36th	600	1,928		2,528
7th	296	1,397		1,693
92nd	176	1,466		1,642
81st	251	973		1,224
6th	93	453		546
88th	29	89		118
Total	47,205	198,056		
Others	3,075	7,634		
Grand total	50,280	205,690		

Diagram 49.—Casualties suffered by each division.

the papers involved in their transfer had been completed. Hence they were reported in their original organizations.

Among the 10,709 " other " casualties there is one most interesting and not inconsiderable group, some of the members of which are included in " troops not in divisions," and the rest among the casualties of replacement and depot divisions. These are the men who deserted to the front. They went A. W. O. L. (absent without leave) from their organizations in the zone of supplies or in the training areas, and found their way up to the battle line, where many of them took part in the fighting and some of them were killed or wounded. These cases were so numerous that Gen. Pershing made special arrangements by which trained men who had rendered good service behind the lines could, as a reward, secure opportunity to go to the front and take part in the fighting.

In the next chapter a more careful analysis is made of American casualties, and the battle and disease deaths in this war are compared with the records of the United States and other nations in previous wars.

SUMMARY.

1. Two out of every three American soldiers who reached France took part in battle. The number who reached France was 2,084,000, and of these 1,390,000 saw active service at the front.

2. Of the 42 divisions that reached France 29 took part in active combat service. Seven of them were Regular Army divisions, 11 were organized from the National Guard, and 11 were made up of National Army troops.

3. American divisions were in battle for 200 days and engaged in 13 major operations.

4. From the middle of August until the end of the war the American divisions held during the greater part of the time a front longer than that held by the British.

5. In October the American divisions held 101 miles of line, or 23 per cent of the entire western front.

6. On the 1st of April the Germans had a superiority of 324,000 in rifle strength. Due to American arrivals the allied strength exceeded that of the Germans in June and was more than 600,000 above it in November.

7. In the Battle of St. Mihiel 550,000 Americans were engaged, as compared with about 100,000 on the Northern side in the Battle of Gettysburg. The artillery fired more than 1,000,000 shells in four hours, which is the most intense concentration of artillery fire recorded in history.

8. The Meuse-Argonne Battle lasted for 47 days, during which 1,200,000 American troops were engaged.

9. The American battle losses of the war were 50,000 killed and 206,000 wounded. They are heavy when counted in terms of lives and suffering, but light compared with the enormous price paid by the nations at whose sides we fought.

Chapter IX.

HEALTH AND CASUALTIES.

THE DEADLIEST WAR.

Of every 100 American soldiers and sailors who took part in the war with Germany, 2 were killed or died of disease during the period of hostilities. In the Northern Army during the Civil War the number was about 10. Among the other great nations in this war, between 20 and 25 in each 100 called to the colors were killed or died. To carry the comparison still further, American losses in this war were relatively one-fifth as large as during the Civil War and less than one-tenth as large as in the ranks of the enemy or among the nations associated with us.

The war was undoubtedly the bloodiest which has ever been fought. One possible competitor might be the Crimean War, in which the casualty rate per 100 men was equally heavy. The British forces in the Crimean War lost 22 of every 100 men, the French 31, the Turkish 27, and the Russian 43. More than four-fifths of the losses were, however, deaths from disease, while in the recent war with Germany disease deaths were inconsiderable as compared with battle deaths. The forces engaged in the Crimean War were, moreover, much smaller.

TABLE 9.—*Battle deaths in armies engaged in present war, 1914–1918.*

Russia	1,700,000
Germany	1,600,000
France	1,385,300
Great Britain	900,000
Austria	800,000
Italy	364,000
Turkey	250,000
Serbia and Montenegro	125,000
Belgium	102,000
Roumania	100,000
Bulgaria	100,000
United States	50,300
Greece	7,000
Portugal	2,000
Total	7,485,600

The total battle deaths in the recent war were greater than all the deaths in all wars for more than 100 years previous. From 1793 to 1914 total deaths in war may safely be estimated at something under 6,000,000. Battle deaths alone from 1914 to 1918 totaled about 7,500,000. An estimate of the losses of the principal nations engaged is shown in Table 9. As the final records are not yet wholly complete, these figures are approximate in some cases. Only deaths

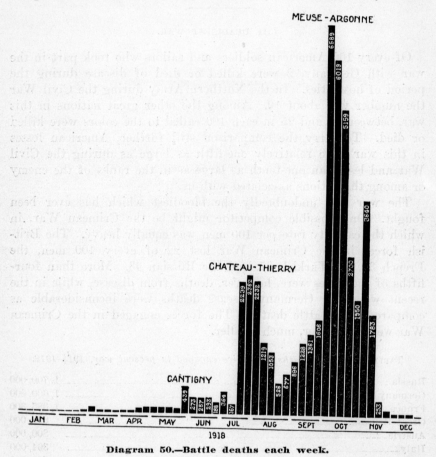

Diagram 50.—Battle deaths each week.

resulting directly from action are included. The total deaths from all causes is very much larger, as some of the armies lost more heavily from diseases and privation than from battle.

The table shows that Russia had the heaviest losses, in spite of the fact that she withdrew from the war after the fall of 1917. American losses are third from the bottom of the list. German losses were thirty-two times as great as the losses of the United States, the French twenty-eight times, and the British eighteen times as large.

That American losses were not more severe is due to the fact that our armies were only in heavy fighting for 200 days. Diagram 50 shows the number of battle deaths occurring each week through 1918. The first rise in the columns, the last part of May, reflects the battle of Cantigny. The second rise, in July, indicates the heavy losses which took place when American divisions were thrown in along the Marne salient at the beginning of the allied offensive. The heaviest losses were in the Meuse-Argonne drive from the last week of September until November 11. The weekly deaths during a part of that period were around the 6,000 mark.

Infantry & Mach.Gun	Officers	80.5
	Men	51.7
Air Service	Officers	33.3
	Men	.6
Engineer Corps	Officers	11.5
	Men	6.5
Tank Corps	Officers	11.5
	Men	5.4
Artillery	Officers	8.1
	Men	5.6
Signal Corps	Officers	3.8
	Men	7.8
Medical Department	Officers	1.7
	Men	1.9
Quartermaster	Officers	1.7
	Men	.3
Cavalry	Officers	0
	Men	1.4
Ordnance	Officers	0
	Men	.1

Diagram 51.—Battle deaths among each thousand officers and men who reached France.

BATTLE DEATHS BY SERVICES.

The chances of death are much heavier in the Infantry than in any other branch of the service. Diagram 51 compares the various services in respect to the chances of death in each. The bars show how many battle deaths there were among each 1,000 men in the various services who reached France. Of each 1,000 enlisted men in the Infantry 52 were killed in action or died of wounds. The officers show a higher rate. The most striking difference between the death rates of officers and men appears in the Air Service. Here the casualties among officers are much higher than among men because in our service all aviators are officers.

WOUNDED, PRISONERS, AND MISSING.

For every man who was killled in battle, six others were wounded, taken prisoner, or reported missing. The total battle casualties in the expeditionary forces are shown in Table 10. The number who died of wounds was only 7 per cent as large as the number who were wounded.' The hospital records show that about 85 per cent of the men sent to hospitals on account of injuries have been returned to duty. About half the wounded were reported as slightly wounded and many of them would not have been recorded as casualties in previous wars. Except for 373 who died, all the prisoners shown in the table have now been returned.

TABLE 10.—*Battle casualties in the American Expeditionary Forces.*

Killed in action	35, 560
Died of wounds	14, 720
Total dead	50, 280
Wounded severely	90, 830
Wounded slightly	80, 480
Wounded, degree undetermined	34, 380
Total wounded	205, 690
Missing in action (Aug. 1, 1919)	46
Taken prisoner	4, 480
Grand total	260, 496

The number of men reported as missing has been steadily reduced from a total of 78,000 to the figure 46 shown in the table. This reduction has gone on without clearing any case as dead except on evidence establishing the fact of death. The total number of cases cleared as presumed dead will be about 1,550. The results of clearing up the records of more than 21,000 cases, exclusive of prisoners, which were reported in the casualty cables to this country, are shown in diagram 52. The largest number have been found in hospitals, while a considerable number have returned to duty after being lost from their units.

The work of the Central Records Office of the American Expeditionary Forces in clearing up the cases of men listed as missing has been more successful than that done in any of the other armies or in any previous great war. The missing lists of the other nations still run into the hundreds of thousands. The most recent figures for France and Great Britain are 264,000 and 121,000, respectively.

BATTLE AND DISEASE LOSSES.

The total number of lives lost in both Army and Navy from the declaration of war to July 1, 1919, is 125,500. Deaths in the Army, including marines attached to it, were 115,660. About two-thirds

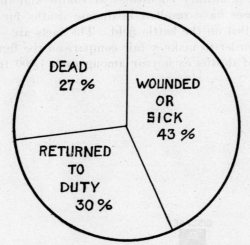

Diagram 52.—Final disposition of cases of men reported missing in action.

of these deaths occurred overseas. Diagram 53 shows the proportion which occurred in the United States and overseas, and also the proportion which disease deaths bore to battle deaths. Under

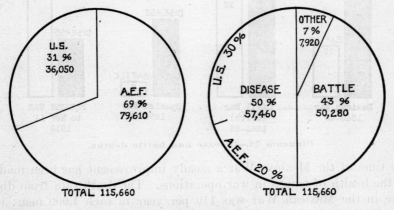

Diagram 53.—Total deaths.

"Other" are included deaths from accident. There were 768 lost at sea, of whom 381 are included under battle deaths, since their loss was the direct result of submarine activity. Almost exactly half the losses were from disease. If the comparison between disease and battle losses is limited to the expeditionary forces, battle losses appear more than twice as large as deaths from disease.

This is the first war in which the United States has been engaged that showed a lower death rate from disease than from battle. In previous wars insanitary conditions at camps and the ravages of epidemic diseases have resulted in disease deaths far in excess of the number killed on the battle field. The facts are shown in diagram 54. In order to make a fair comparison the figures used are the numbers of deaths each year among each 1,000 troops. Since

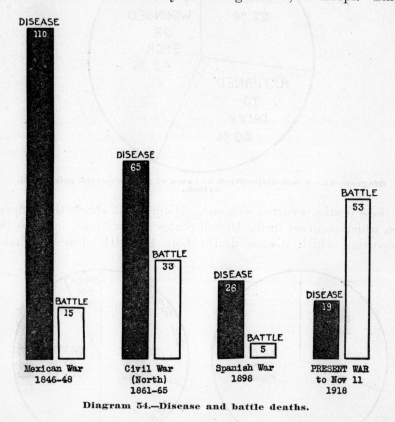

Diagram 54.—Disease and battle deaths.

the time of the Mexican War a steady improvement has been made in the health of troops in war operations. The death rate from disease in the Mexican War was 110 per year in each 1,000 men; in the Civil War this was reduced to 65; and in the Spanish War to 26; while the rate in the expeditionary forces in this war was 19. The battle rate of 53 for the overseas forces is higher than in any previous war. It is higher than in the Civil War because all of the fighting was concentrated in one year, while in the Civil War it stretched over four years. The rates in this war for the total forces under arms both in the United States and France from the beginning of the war to May 1, 1919, were 13 for battle and 15 for disease.

THE CONTROL OF DISEASE.

Some of the outstanding causes of the remarkably low disease death rate in the war against Germany are: (1) A highly trained medical personnel, (2) compulsory vaccination of the entire Army against typhoid fever, (3) thorough camp sanitation and control of drinking water, and (4) adequate provision of hospital facilities.

There were at the beginning of the war 2,089 commissioned medical officers, including the Reserves. During the war 31,251 physicians from civil life were commissioned in the Medical Corps. This number included leaders of medical science who have not only made possible the application of the most recent advances of medicine in the prevention and cure of disease, but have themselves made new discoveries during the course of the war, resulting in great saving of life in our own and other armies.

The intestinal diseases such as dysentery, the typhoids, bubonic plague, cholera, and typhus, have ravaged and even obliterated armies in the past. During the Spanish-American War typhoid fever alone caused 85 per cent of the total number of deaths. In the War with Germany these diseases have been practically eliminated as causes of death. Diagram 55 shows the relative proportion of deaths caused by principal diseases. During the entire war up to May 1, 1919, a total of only 2,328 cases of typhoid fever have been reported and only 227 deaths from this cause. The result is due to the compulsory vaccination of every man who entered the Army and to excellent sanitary conditions. The other intestinal diseases are similarly of little effect as causes of death or have not occurred at all.

It was to be expected that with careful control exercised, epidemics of these diseases would be avoided in the United States; but in the Expeditionary Forces, where troops were quartered in temporary camps, billeted with civilians, or actively engaged in prolonged battle, the reduction of these diseases is a notable achievement in sanitary control.

It is evident from the diagram that pneumonia has been the greatest cause of death. More than 40,000 died of the disease. Of these, probably 25,000 resulted from the influenza-pneumonia pandemic which swept through every camp and cantonment in this country and caused thousands of deaths in the expeditionary forces. Up to September 14, 1918, only 9,840 deaths from disease had occurred in the Army, and the death rate for the period of the war up to that time was only 5 per year for each 1,000 men. During the eight weeks from September 14 to the 8th of November 316,089 cases of influenza and 53,449 of pneumonia were reported among troops in this country. The explosive character of the epidemic is shown in diagram 56. The curve in the diagram shows the weekly death rate for each 1,000 troops in this country during the year 1918. The curve starts to rise sharply during the third week in September. It reached its high point the second week in October, when 4 out of each 1,000 troops under arms in this country died. The rate subsided at the end of October, but during the succeeding months remained somewhat higher than it had been previous to the epidemic.

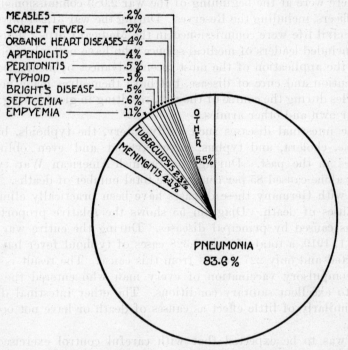

MEASLES————.2%
SCARLET FEVER————.3%
ORGANIC HEART DISEASES—4%
APPENDICITIS————4%
PERITONITIS————.5%
TYPHOID————.5%
BRIGHT'S DISEASE————.5%
SEPTCEMIA————.6%
EMPYEMIA————11%
OTHER 5.5%
TUBERCULOSIS 2.3%
MENINGITIS 4.1%
PNEUMONIA 83.6%

Diagram 55.—Deaths by principal diseases.

Two other diseases which offered difficult problems for the medical force were measles and spinal meningitis. Measles was prevalent during the first year of the war and was particularly dangerous as the predecessor of pneumonia. After vigorous efforts to control it, the number of cases was greatly reduced. Meningitis has caused nearly 2,000 deaths, ranking next to pneumonia as shown in diagram 55. Both of these contagious diseases were largely the result of bringing numbers of men together in the confinement of camps and cantonments where the control of contagion is difficult. In the case of measles, men from rural communities who had not been immunized by previous exposure were particularly susceptible.

VENEREAL DISEASE.

Great success has also been experienced in the control of the venereal diseases. A comprehensive program of education, together with medical prophylaxis, has produced unusual results. While these diseases have continued to be the most frequent cause of admissions to the sick report, and the greatest source of nonef-

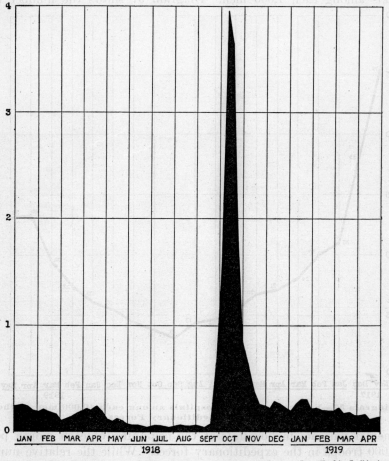

Diagram 56.—Deaths per 1,000 soldiers each week in the United States, showing effect of influenza epidemic.

fectiveness in the Army, a large proportion of the cases were contracted before entering the Army. A special study of all new cases of venereal diseases reported at five large cantonments, Lee, Va.; Dix, N. J.; Upton, N. Y.; Meade, Md.; and Pike, Ark., during the year ended May 21, 1919, shows that of 48,167 cases treated, 96 per cent were contracted before entering the Army and only 4 per cent after.

The record for the forces overseas has been particularly noteworthy. There, few fresh recruits entered the Army from civil
life, and hence the conditions more accurately show the effects of
the Army control exercised.

Up to September, 1918, there was steady reduction of noneffective-
ness from venereal diseases in the Army overseas. At the beginning of that month there was less than one venereal patient in hospitals among each 1,000 men. Diagram 57 shows the number of

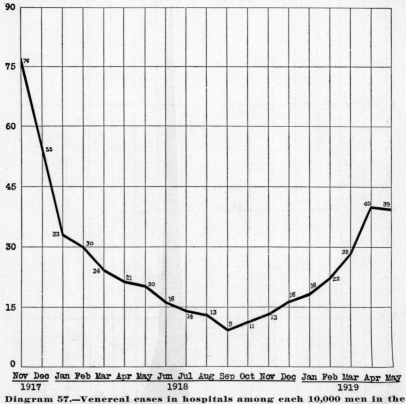

Diagram 57.—Venereal cases in hospitals among each 10,000 men in the
American Expeditionary Forces.

venereal patients in hospitals at the beginning of each month per
10,000 troops in the expeditionary forces. While the relative number of patients has increased since hostilities stopped, the record is
still excellent. Regular weekly inspections, covering about 85 per
cent of the total number of troops overseas, have disclosed during
six months since the armistice less than one new case in each thousand
men examined weekly. The actual average was one new case each
week among each 2,630 men examined.

HOSPITALIZATION.

At the beginning of the war what was then considered an extrava-
gant program of hospital construction was entered upon, with the

intent that in no case should the Army lack facilities for the care of its sick.   Table 11 summarizes the hospital construction in the United States.

TABLE 11.—*Army hospital construction in the United States.*

	Number.	Normal bed capacity.
New hospitals	62	88,468
Leased buildings and converted Army posts	39	29,383
Post hospitals remodeled	48	6,056
Total	149	123,907

The figures are exclusive of very numerous small hospitals already in Army use.   In addition more than 200 hospitals were put in oper-

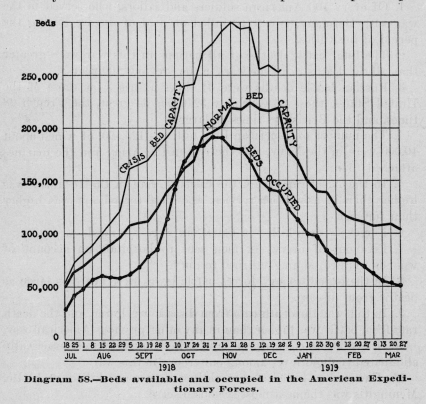

Diagram 58.—**Beds available and occupied in the American Expeditionary Forces.**

ation overseas.   On December 1, 1918, there were available in Army hospitals 399,510 beds, or 1 bed to every 9 men in the Army.   Of these, 287,290 were overseas and 112,220 were in this country.

Diagram 58 shows the number of patients at the end of each week in the American Expeditionary Forces compared with the beds available.   The hospital capacity was exceeded in this country only during the influenza epidemic, when it became necessary to take over barracks for hospital purposes. The overseas record was even better. Except during two weeks in October, at the height of the attack on the Hindenburg line, the number of patients did not exceed the normal bed capacity of the hospitals, and at that time there were approximately 60,000 unused emergency beds.

Over 130,000 patients have been evacuated from the expeditionary forces to hospitals in this country. They have been distributed to hospitals in this country in accordance with a twofold plan permitting the specialization of hospitals for the most efficient treatment of the various kinds of cases and placing the convalescents near their homes.

SUMMARY.

1. Of every 100 American soldiers and sailors, who served in the war with Germany, two were killed or died of disease during the period of hositilties.

2. The total battle deaths of all nations in this war were greater than all the deaths in all the wars in the previous 100 years.

3. Russian battle deaths were 34 times as heavy as those of the United States, those of Germany 32 times as great, the French 28 times, and the British 18 times as large.

4. The number of American lives lost was 125,500, of which about 10,000 were in the Navy, and the rest in the Army and the marines attached to it.

5. In the American Army the casualty rate in the Infantry was higher than in any other service, and that for officers was higher than for men.

6. For every man killed in battle six were wounded.

7. Five out of every six men sent to hospitals on account of wounds were cured and returned to duty.

8. In the expeditionary forces battle losses were twice as large as deaths from disease.

9. In this war the death rate from disease was lower, and the death rate from battle was higher than in any other previous American war.

10. Inoculation, clean camps, and safe drinking water, practically eliminated typhoid fever among our troops in this war.

11. Pneumonia killed more soldiers than were killed in battle. Meningitis was the next most serious disease.

12. Of each 100 cases of venereal disease recorded in the United States, 96 were contracted before entering the Army and only 4 afterwards.

13. During the entire war available hospital facilities in the American Expeditionary Forces have been in excess of the needs.

Chapter X.

A MILLION DOLLARS AN HOUR.

TOTAL WAR EXPENDITURES.

For a period of 25 months, from April, 1917, through April, 1919, the war cost the United States considerably more than $1,000,000 an hour. Treasury disbursements during the period reached a total of $23,500,000,000, of which $1,650,000,000 may be charged to the normal expenses which would have occurred in time of peace. The balance may be counted as the direct money cost of the war to the end of April, 1919, a sum of $21,850,000,000. The figure is 20 times the prewar national debt. It is nearly large enough to pay the entire costs of our Government from 1791 up to the outbreak of the European war. Our expenditure in this war was sufficient to have carried on the Revolutionary War continuously for more than a thousand years at the rate of expenditure which that war actually involved.

In addition to this huge expenditure loans were advanced to the Allies at the rate of nearly half a million dollars an hour. Congress authorized for this purpose $10,000,000,000, and there was actually paid to various Governments the sum of $8,850,000,000.

Of the United States Government war costs, the Army was responsible for the expenditure of 64 per cent, or just short of two-thirds of the entire amount. Through April 30, 1919, there had been withdrawn from the Treasury on the Army account $14,244,061,000. If there is deducted from this figure what would be the normal expediture for a peace-time Army for a similar period there remains a total of $13,930,000,000 directly chargeable to the war.

The rate of expenditure for the Army and for the entire Government increased rapidly as the war progressed. This is illustrated in diagram 59, which compares the daily rates of expenditure for the first three months of the war, the fiscal year entirely included in the war, and the first 10 months of the current fiscal year. The total height of the columns shows the daily rate of expenditure for the whole Government and the solid portion of the column the rate for the Army.

During the first three months war expenditures were at the rate of $2,000,000 per day. During the next year they averaged more than $22,000,000 a day. For the final 10 months of the period the

131

daily total reached the enormous sum of over $44,000,000. The very high daily average in the last period, most of which is in the months after the termination of hostilities, is surprising until we consider that the building of ships for the Emergency Fleet Corporation, the construction and operation of naval vessels, the food,

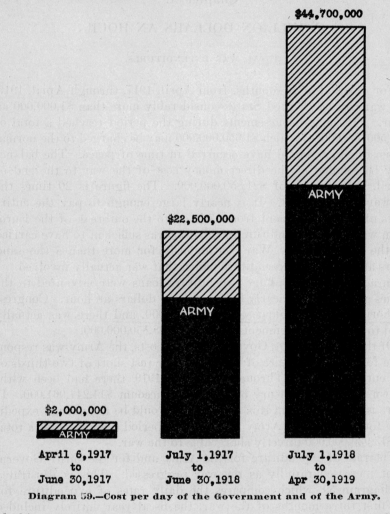

Diagram 59.—Cost per day of the Government and of the Army.

clothing, pay, and land and ocean transportation of the Army have had to go forward at about the same rate as during the war. The great flow of munitions and supplies for the Army and Navy could not, out of regard for the industrial balance of the country, be stopped with too great abruptness. A considerable number of war-time activities and purchases had still to be paid for as well.

ARMY EXPENDITURES.

Table 12 shows the amounts expended by each important Army bureau. The Quartermaster Corps, which paid the soldiers and furnished them with food, clothing, equipment, and miscellaneous supplies, spent the most. The Ordnance Department was next in order, with over $4,000,000,000 for munitions, more than half of its expenditure being for artillery ammunition.

TABLE 12.—*Expenditures by Army bureaus.*

	Expended to Apr. 30, 1919.	Per cent.
Quartermaster Corps:		
Pay of the Army, etc.	$1,831,273,000	12.9
Other Quartermaster Corps appropriations	6,242,745,000	43.8
Ordnance Department	4,087,347,000	28.7
Air Service	859,291,000	6.0
Engineer Corps	638,974,000	4.5
Medical Department	314,544,000	2.2
Signal Corps	128,920,000	.9
Chemical Warfare Service	83,299,000	.6
Provost Marshal General	[1] 24,301,000	.17
Secretary's office and miscellaneous	[1] 33,367,000	.23
Total	14,244,061,000	100.00

[1] Figures are for Dec. 31, 1918. Expenditures since that date for these purposes have been small compared with other items in table.

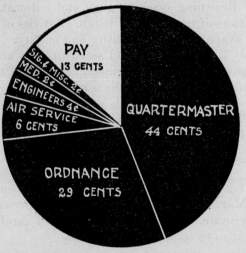

Diagram 60.—Where the Army dollar went.

The total of our Army expenditures shown in Table 12 about equals the value of all the gold produced in the whole world from the discovery of America up to the outbreak of the European war. The single item of pay for the Army is larger than the combined salaries of all the public-school principals and teachers in the United States for the five years from 1912 to 1916.

WHERE THE DOLLAR WENT.

Diagram 60 shows the relative amount of the Army expenditures spent for different purposes. It does this by dividing the typical dollar into sectors, showing the number of cents of each dollar that went for each purpose.

PERMANENT ASSETS.

As a result of the war efforts large quantities of munitions, supplies, and equipment have been secured which will be of value for many years to come. The Army now owns some of the finest docks in the world. The 16 National Army cantonments and 3 of the National Guard camps will be retained permanently as training camps. A number of first-class aviation fields and depots and balloon schools will be a permanent asset. We have stocks of most articles of clothing sufficient to last our Army for a number of years. There is a large supply of standardized trucks.

As to rifles and machine guns and their ammunition, light and heavy artillery and ammunition, tanks and tractors, of these we have a supply more than sufficient to equip fully an army of a million men and maintain them in active combat for six months. These munitions are of the best quality and latest design—Springfield and Enfield rifles; Browning machine guns and automatic rifles; field guns and howitzers of tried French design. Articles of miscellaneous equipment are available in like quantity and quality.

Thousands of Liberty motors and service planes are immediately available for any emergency. Engineer, signal, and medical equipment is on hand to the value of millions of dollars.

All these are lasting assets which we have as a result of war expenditures. They give us a most valuable equipment for preparedness in the Military Establishment.

WAR EXPENDITURES OF ALL NATIONS.

Table 13 gives the figures showing the war expenditures of all nations up to May, 1919. It is as yet too soon to present figures that are entirely accurate, but these data have been carefully compiled and are believed to be substantially reliable.

TABLE 13.—*Estimated total war expenditures of principal nations to Apr. 30, 1919.*

[All figures in billions of dollars and excluding normal expenses and loans to allies.]

Country.	Billions of dollars.
Great Britain and Dominions	38
France	26
United States	22
Russia	18
Italy	13
Belgium, Roumania, Portugal, Jugo-Slavia	5
Japan and Greece	1
Total allies and United States	123
Germany	39
Austria-Hungary	21
Turkey and Bulgaria	3
Total Teutonic allies	63
Grand total	186

The total direct war costs amount to about $186,000,000,000, and of this sum the enemy countries spent about one-third and those on the allied side about two-thirds. Germany spent more than any other nation, and was closely followed by Great Britain, whose expenditures include those of her colonies. The figure for France is $12,000,000,000 less than that for Great Britain, and our own figure is below that for France. The Austrian expenditure was almost equal to that of the United States. It is noteworthy that the United States spent about one-eighth of the entire cost of the war and something less than one-fifth of the expenditures on the allied side.

SUMMARY.

1. The war cost the United States considerably more than $1,000,000 an hour for over two years.

2. The direct cost was about $22,000,000,000, or nearly enough to pay the entire cost of running the United States Government from 1791 up to the outbreak of the European war.

3. Our expenditures in this war were sufficient to have carried on the Revolutionary War continuously for more than 1,000 years at the rate of expenditure which that war actually involved.

4. In addition to this huge expenditure nearly $10,000,000,000 have been loaned by the United States to the Allies.

5. The Army expenditures have been over $14,000,000,000, or nearly two-thirds of our total war costs.

6. During the first three months our war expenditures were at the rate of $2,000,000 per day. During the next year they averaged more

than $22,000,000 a day. For the final 10 months of the period, from April, 1917, to April, 1919, the daily average was over $44,000,000.

7. Although the Army expenditures are less than two-thirds of our total war costs, they are nearly equal to the value of all the gold produced in the whole world from the discovery of America up to the outbreak of the European war.

8. The pay of the Army during the war cost more than the combined salaries of all the public-school principals and teachers in the United States for the five years from 1912 to 1916.

⌐ 9. The total war costs of all nations were about $186,000,000,000, of which the Allies and the United States spent two-thirds and the enemy one-third.

10. The three nations spending the greatest amounts were Germany, Great Britain, and France, in that order. After them come the United States and Austria-Hungary, with substantially equal expenditures.

⟍ 11. The United States spent about one-eighth of the entire cost of the war, and something less than one-fifth of the expenditures of the allied side.

SOME INTERNATIONAL COMPARISONS.

TABLE 14.—*Duration of the war.*

Allied and associated nations.	War declared by Central Powers.	War declared against Central Powers.	Duration of war.		
			Years.	Months.	Days.
1. Serbia	July 28, 1914	Aug. 9, 1914	4	3	14
2. Russia[1]	Aug. 1, 1914	Nov. 3, 1914	3	7	3
3. France	Aug. 3, 1914	Aug. 3, 1914	4	3	8
4. Belgium	Aug. 4, 1914	Apr. 7, 1917	4	3	7
5. Great Britain	Nov. 23, 1914	Aug. 4, 1914	4	3	7
6. Montenegro	Aug. 9, 1914	Aug. 6, 1914	4	3	5
7. Japan	Aug. 27, 1914	Aug. 23, 1914	4	2	19
8. Portugal	Mar. 9, 1916	Nov. 23, 1914	3	11	19
9. Italy		May 23, 1915	3	5	19
10. San Marino		June 6, 1915	3	5	4
11. Roumania[2]	Aug. 29, 1916	Aug. 27, 1916	1	6	10
12. Greece		Nov. 23, 1916	1	11	18
13. United States		Apr. 6, 1917	1	7	5
14. Panama		Apr. 7, 1917	1	7	4
15. Cuba		Apr. 7, 1917	1	7	4
16. Siam		July 22, 1917	1	3	20
17. Liberia		Aug. 4, 1917	1	3	8
18. China		Aug. 14, 1917	1	2	28
19. Brazil		Oct. 26, 1917	1		16
20. Guatemala		Apr. 21, 1918		6	21
21. Nicaragua		May 6, 1918		6	5
22. Haiti		July 12, 1918		3	30
23. Honduras		July 19, 1918		3	23

[1] Treaty Mar. 3, 1918. [2] Treaty Mar. 6, 1918.

137

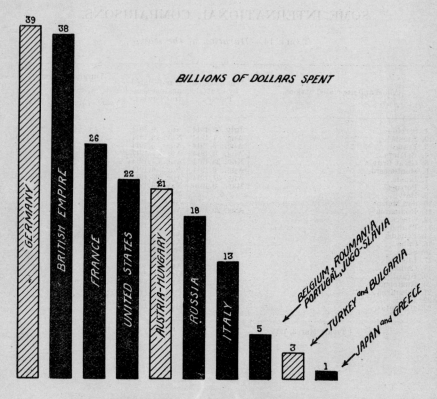

TOTAL EXPENDITURES $186,000,000,000

Diagram 61.—Billions of dollars spent by each nation for direct war
expenses to the spring of 1919.

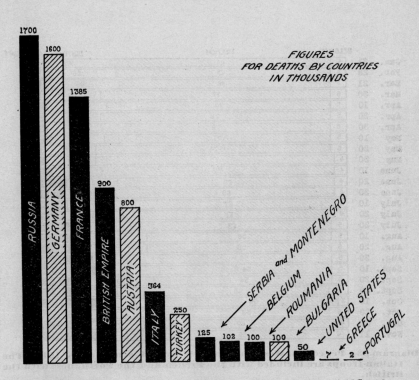

FIGURES
FOR DEATHS BY COUNTRIES
IN THOUSANDS

BATTLE DEATHS OF ARMIES ENGAGED IN PRESENT WAR 7,485,000

Diagram 62.—Thousands of men killed in action and died of wounds.

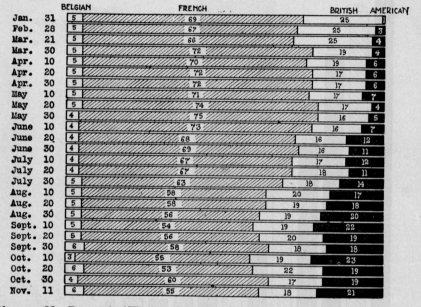

		BELGIAN	FRENCH	BRITISH	AMERICAN
Jan.	31	5	69	25	
Feb.	28	5	67	25	3
Mar.	21	5	66	25	4
Mar.	30	5	72	19	4
Apr.	10	5	70	19	6
Apr.	20	5	72	17	6
Apr.	30	5	72	17	6
May	10	5	71	17	7
May	20	5	74	17	4
May	30	4	75	16	5
June	10	4	73	16	7
June	20	4	68	16	12
June	30	4	69	16	11
July	10	4	67	17	12
July	20	4	67	18	11
July	30	5	63	18	14
Aug.	10	5	58	20	17
Aug.	20	5	58	19	18
Aug.	30	5	56	19	20
Sept.	10	5	54	19	22
Sept.	20	5	56	20	19
Sept.	30	6	58	18	18
Oct.	10	3	55	19	23
Oct.	20	6	53	22	19
Oct.	30	4	60	17	19
Nov.	11	6	55	18	21

Diagram 63.—Per cent of Western front held by each army during 1918. The Italian troops are included with the French and the Portuguese with the British.

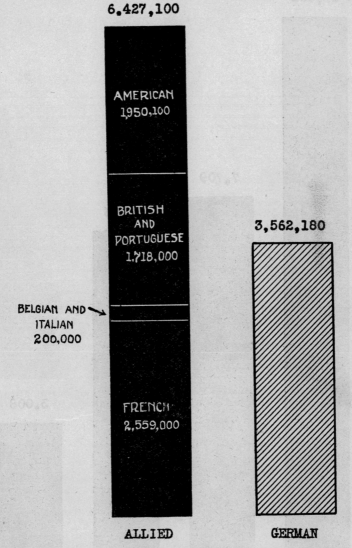

6,427,100

AMERICAN
1,950,100

BRITISH
AND
PORTUGUESE
1,718,000

3,562,180

BELGIAN AND
ITALIAN
200,000

FRENCH
2,559,000

ALLIED   GERMAN

Diagram 64.—Ration strength of the allied and enemy forces on the
Western front at the time of the armistice.

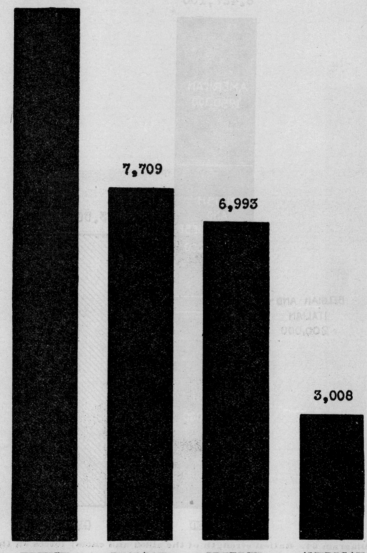

Diagram 65.—Guns organized in batteries at the date of the armistice.

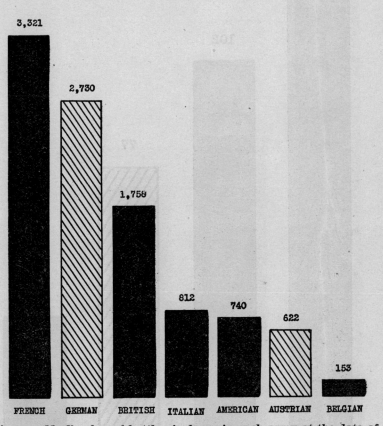

Diagram 66.—Number of battle airplanes in each army at the date of the armistice.

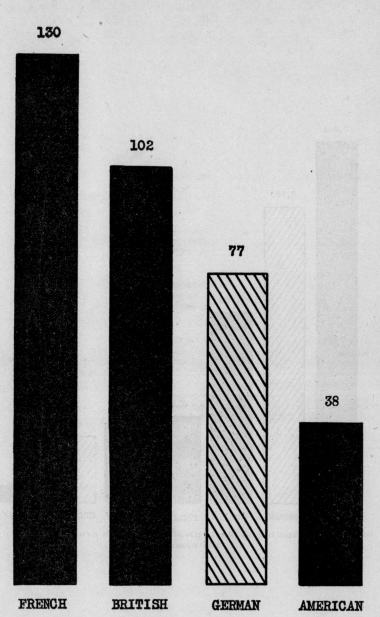

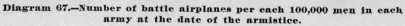

Diagram 67.—Number of battle airplanes per each 100,000 men in each army at the date of the armistice.

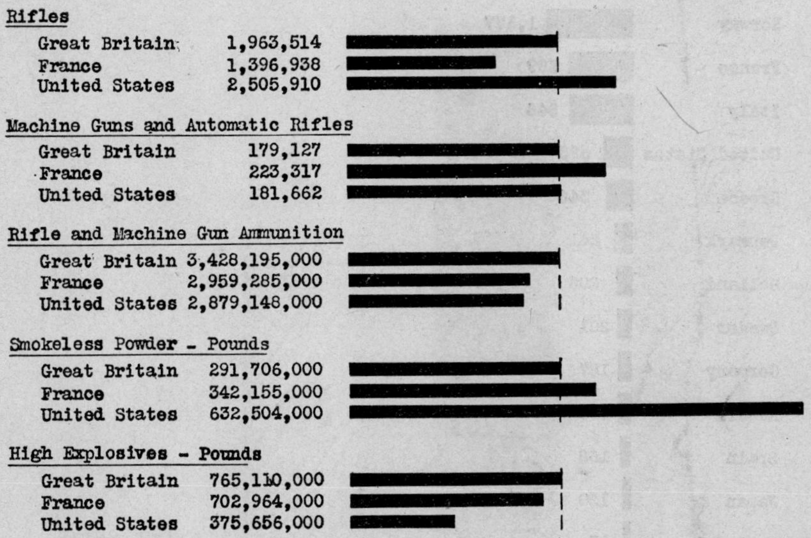

Rifles

Great Britain	1,963,514
France	1,396,938
United States	2,505,910

Machine Guns and Automatic Rifles

Great Britain	179,127
France	223,317
United States	181,662

Rifle and Machine Gun Ammunition

Great Britain	3,428,195,000
France	2,959,285,000
United States	2,879,148,000

Smokeless Powder - Pounds

Great Britain	291,706,000
France	342,155,000
United States	632,504,000

High Explosives - Pounds

Great Britain	765,110,000
France	702,964,000
United States	375,656,000

Diagram 68.—Production of articles of ordnance by Great Britain, France, and the United States during the 19 months of American participation from Apr. 6, 1917, to Nov. 11, 1918.

132966°—19——10

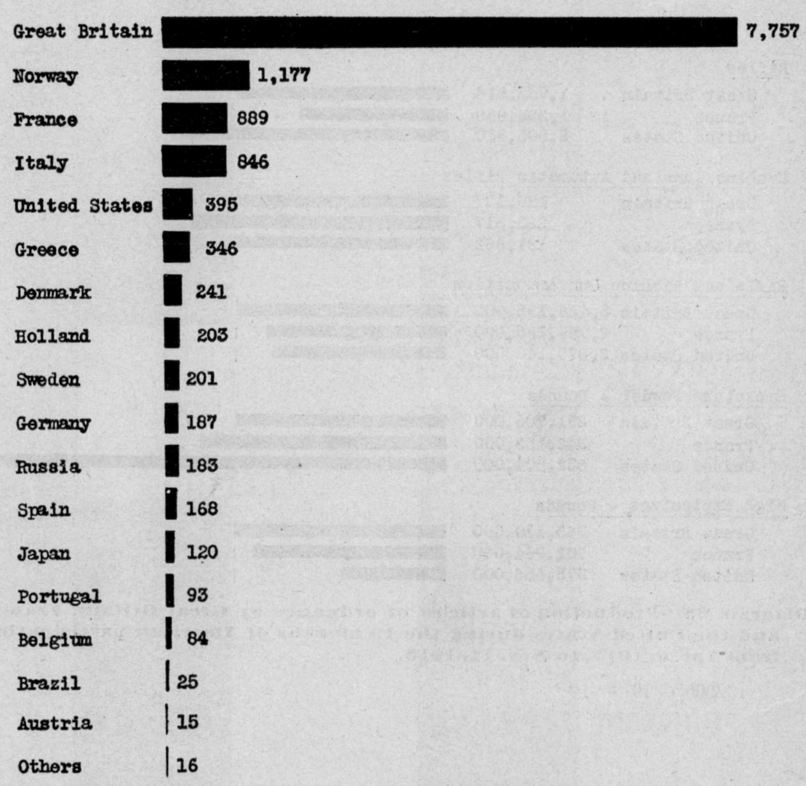

Great Britain	7,757
Norway	1,177
France	889
Italy	846
United States	395
Greece	346
Denmark	241
Holland	203
Sweden	201
Germany	187
Russia	183
Spain	168
Japan	120
Portugal	93
Belgium	84
Brazil	25
Austria	15
Others	16

Diagram 69.—Thousands of gross tons of merchant shipping lost
through acts of war.

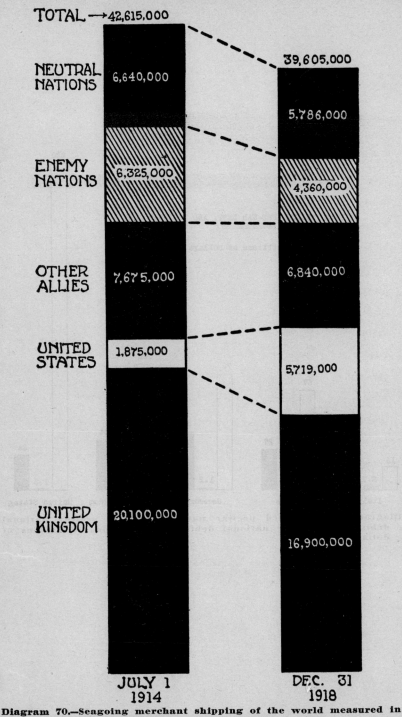

TOTAL → 42,615,000

39,605,000

NEUTRAL NATIONS 6,640,000

5,786,000

ENEMY NATIONS 6,325,000

4,360,000

OTHER ALLIES 7,675,000

6,840,000

UNITED STATES 1,875,000

5,719,000

UNITED KINGDOM 20,100,000

16,900,000

JULY 1
1914

DEC. 31
1918

Diagram 70.—Seagoing merchant shipping of the world measured in
gross tons on July 1, 1914, and Dec. 31, 1918.

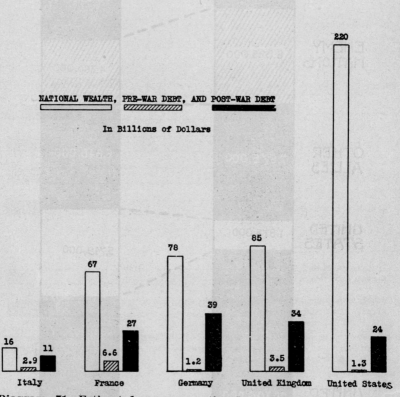

NATIONAL WEALTH, PRE-WAR DEBT, AND POST-WAR DEBT

In Billions of Dollars

Diagram 71.—Estimated prewar national wealth, prewar national debts, and postwar national debts of five nations in billions of dollars.

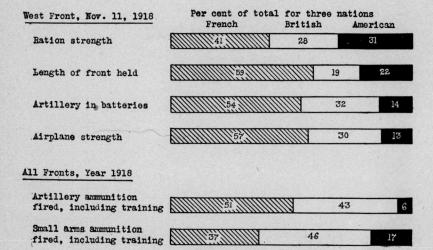

West Front, Nov. 11, 1918

Per cent of total for three nations

	French	British	American
Ration strength	41	28	31
Length of front held	59	19	22
Artillery in batteries	54	32	14
Airplane strength	57	30	13

All Fronts, Year 1918

	French	British	American
Artillery ammunition fired, including training	51	43	6
Small arms ammunition fired, including training	37	46	17

Diagram 72.—Comparative strength of French, British, and American Armies at the signing of the armistice and comparative expenditures of ammunition during 1918.

INDEX.